STEVEN SODERBERGH

INTERVIEWS

CONVERSATIONS WITH FILMMAKERS SERIES

PETER BRUNETTE, GENERAL EDITOR

STEVEN
SODERBERGH

INTERVIEWS

EDITED BY ANTHONY KAUFMAN

UNIVERSITY PRESS OF MISSISSIPPI / JACKSON

www.upress.state.ms.us

10 09 08 07 06 05 04 03 02   4 3 2 1
∞
Library of Congress Cataloging-in-Publication Data

Steven Soderbergh : interviews / edited by Anthony Kaufman.
    p. cm.
    Includes index.
    ISBN 1-57806-428-7 (cloth : alk. paper). —ISBN 1-57806-429-5 (pbk. : alk. paper)
    1. Soderbergh, Steven, 1963–   —Interviews.   2. Motion picture producers and
directors—United States—Interviews.   I. Kaufman, Anthony.
PN1998.3.S593 A5 2001
791.43'0233'092—dc21   2001026906

British Library Cataloging-in-Publication Data available

CONTENTS

INTRODUCTION

''I'M STILL A SCHMUCK LIKE EVERYBODY ELSE,'' Steven
Soderbergh told Terri Minsky in one of the director's first interviews, a
lengthy profile that appeared in *Rolling Stone*'s annual Hot issue in May
1989—the month that also certified Soderbergh's breakout success with his
win of the Cannes Film Festival's top prize, the Palme d'Or, for his debut
feature *sex, lies, and videotape*. In the interview, the twenty-six-year-old
filmmaker emerges as self-effacing, cynical, and full of attitude—just the type
that the media and audiences would hope for in a brassy new American
auteur.

But Steven Soderbergh did not conform to expectations. He did not fulfill
the bad boy role of young turk, nor follow in the footsteps of a Woody Allen,
Mike Nichols, or Steven Spielberg, just a few of the filmmakers he was com-
pared with early in his career. Soderbergh followed his own path and, after
just ten feature films, has amassed one of the most eclectic résumés in all of
contemporary American cinema. Whether it be the outrageous adventures
of *Kafka* and *Schizopolis* or the assured dramas of *Erin Brockovich* and *Traffic*,
or just about everything in-between, Soderbergh's oeuvre defies auteurism,
takes on surprising shifts like few before him, and finds the once wry independent "schmuck" transformed into one of Hollywood's foremost hired
guns.

This collection of interviews could easily be subtitled "The Rise and Fall
and Rise of an American Director." Soderbergh goes from "flavor of the
month" with *sex, lies, and videotape* to an enigmatic stumbler in just two
years. The American press virtually ignores his audacious second film *Kafka*,

and then he regains a glimmer of hope with his next work, the subtle coming-of-age film *King of the Hill*. Soderbergh's fourth film *The Underneath*, an adaptation of Robert Siodmak's 1949 film *Criss Cross*, could be called the end of the first phase of Soderbergh's career. Though Soderbergh appears confident with the aesthetic choices he made while shooting *The Underneath* in interviews in 1995, there are clues that indicate Soderbergh's frustration with the direction of his work. "In fifteen years, people will look back at my first four films and they will realize that they were just a preface to a book that I am only now starting to write," he tells Michel Ciment and Hubert Niogret of French film journal *Positif*. "In a way, what I want to do will look a lot like the short films I made when I was young."

That's exactly what Soderbergh accomplishes with his next project, the stripped-down *Schizopolis*, which kicked off a rebirth of Soderbergh's filmmaking that has lasted to this day. In a lengthy 1997 biographical expose in the *Los Angeles Times* titled, "The Funk of Steven Soderbergh,"[1] with the vivid subhead, "His First Film, *sex, lies, and videotape*, Put Him on Top of Hollywood's Hill. He Predicted That It Was All Downhill from There. Why Was He Right?" Scott Collins finds the director at a crossroads, having just finished the difficult, but regenerative task of shooting *Schizopolis* and not sure where to turn for his next directorial task. Soderbergh echoes the same sentiments that were only hinted at during the *Positif* interview, but with further and more chilling detail. "To sit on a movie set at age thirty-one and wonder whether or not you even want to do this, having no other real skills, is so terrifying and depressing," he says. Although Soderbergh says elsewhere he felt better than ever after the creative outburst that was *Schizopolis*, Collins paints him in a far more ominous light: The article ends with Soderbergh foreseeing his own early death in a plane crash.

In the *Schizopolis* interviews that appear here, however, there is little of the gloom and doom that appeared in the *L.A. Times*. Soderbergh is less serious, and more thrilled with *Schizopolis'* ultra-low budget, freewheeling style. "I needed a lark," he tells Patricia Thomson in *The Independent Film and Video Monthly* in late 1996, after festival screenings at Toronto and the Hamptons where Soderbergh's dual energizing efforts *Schizopolis* and *Gray's Anat-*

---

[1] Scott Collins, "The Funk of Steven Soderbergh: His First Film, *sex, lies, and videotape*, Put Him on Top of Hollywood's Hill. He Predicted Then That It Was All Downhill from There. Why Was He Right?," *Los Angeles Times*, February 6, 1997.

omy—an adaptation of Spalding Gray's monologue—were screened. "I think what will happen is I'll end up applying a lot of things that I got out of *Schizopolis* to something a little less schizophrenic," he continues. From super-structured to schizophrenia, Soderbergh's subsequent films all seem to benefit from this turning point in his thinking. Throughout his career and throughout this book, in fact, Soderbergh cites *Schizopolis* as a source of inspiration.

In the interviews post-*Schizopolis*, a reinvigorated Soderbergh comes forward, echoing the humor and lack of pretension in his first *sex, lies* conversations where the dialogue is considerably more focused on his own sex life than serious filmmaking. "The trick was finding that right balance between not fucking it up and staying loose," he tells the *Village Voice*'s Dennis Lim about 1998's *Out of Sight,* the George Clooney/Jennifer Lopez film that attracted Hollywood attention and garnered Soderbergh his first entrance into the mainstream. In the *Out of Sight* interviews here by Lim, *Film Journal International*'s Ed Kelleher, and the *LA Weekly*'s Paul Malcolm, Soderbergh continues to reflect on the stimulating aspects of *Schizopolis,* but he also discusses his new entry into Hollywood filmmaking, the star power of Clooney and Lopez and the importance of the genre film to his once again burgeoning career.

With his next film *The Limey,* Soderbergh begins to comment on another important element in his career, British director Richard Lester *(A Hard Day's Night),* with whom Soderbergh collaborated on the irreverent Faber and Faber book *Getting Away with It.* Combining interviews between Lester and Soderbergh, and diaries from a particularly difficult moment in Soderbergh's career right after finishing *The Underneath,* the book figures as an important part of the director's creative output. In an interview following the publication of *Getting Away with It* in Salon.com, Michael Sragow speaks with Soderbergh extensively about his renewal, reflecting on the career pitfalls that plagued him and what efforts he took to combat his lack of enthusiasm for filmmaking after making *The Underneath.* With no specific film to plug, the interview serves as a significant and candid snapshot of the director's thoughts on the eve of the year 2000—the year that thrust Soderbergh into a spotlight not seen since *sex, lies, and videotape.*

With the combined reinforcement of Soderbergh's own experiments and the muse of Richard Lester boosting his confidence, *The Limey,* brings out similar discussions of Soderbergh's creative renaissance. With each new criti-

cally lauded film thereafter, the conversations included here trace Soderbergh's new acclaim, his near burn-out years before, and what he has learned
throughout the dips and hops in the process. "If you can't hit the three-
point shot," Soderbergh told me in an interview for *indieWIRE* at the end of
2000, "you should stop shooting three-point shots, and learn how to drive
the lane. So I'm just trying to play to my strengths."

What are the strengths of a director who seemingly defies labeling? Is it
possible to find a through line when looking over this collection of interviews? One of the common threads, ironically, is that very struggle to define
his work. Nearly every interview touches on Soderbergh's unpredictability
and eclecticism. As early as 1993, Soderbergh is certain that he is not one of
Andrew Sarris's auteurs, but a much more conventional storyteller, uninter-
ested in imposing a "style" on to the stories he directs. "A Huston or a Hawks
were never fashionable, and they expressed themselves through a variety of
genres," he explains in an interview in *Positif*. "I'm not a visionary artist;
sometimes I would like to be, but I don't belong to that category of filmmakers like Kubrick, Altman, or Fellini. . . . I am not trying to impose my style."
Whether it's the colorful, almost surreal *King of the Hill* or the handheld,
edgy *Traffic*, Soderbergh remains persistent in refusing the auteur's mantle.
After making *Kafka*, for instance, Soderbergh confesses to *Positif*, "I know
that some people had imagined an entire career for me because of *sex, lie,
and videotape*. According to them, I should have shot a certain type of film,
but I knew I wouldn't. So I thought that I might as well disappoint them
right away by making something completely different."

Yet as difficult as it is to pin down the elusive Steven Soderbergh, certain
threads do become apparent throughout these interviews. Most pronounced
is the Soderbergh protagonist: alienated, isolated, estranged, outsider, underdog. Whether it is the sullen voyeur of *sex, lies*, the disenfranchised gambler
of *The Underneath*, *The Limey* in Los Angeles, or a mother of two in the class
action courts in *Erin Brockovich*, Soderbergh returns to his loner-protagonist
again and again. Comparing *sex, lies, and videotape* to the seemingly antithet-
ical *Kafka*, Soderbergh describes both the characters as "alienated and disoriented." And after making *King of the Hill*, again he indicates his interest in
"main characters that are out of sync with their environment"—a phrase
virtually repeated several years later when speaking with *Premiere Magazine*'s
Anne Thompson about the character of Erin Brockovich.

While Soderbergh's interest in these alienated characters runs through the text, his own direct "personal" connection to the characters grows more distant. In the *sex, lies* interviews, Soderbergh conveys information about his personal life and how it relates to the characters, but as the interviews in the book progress, the direct link between him and his estranged protagonists becomes more obscure. When discussing *sex, lies, and videotape,* many critics tend to equate Soderbergh with the character of Graham (played by James Spader), the impotent liar who videotapes women's confessions. And many of the interviews relate Soderbergh's own problems with women and communication. "The parallels between the director and Graham are far more provocative (and obvious)," writes Katherine Dieckmann, listing a litany of comparisons in a 1989 *Village Voice* story where she spent time with Soderbergh in his then home of Virginia.

But in most of the other films, Soderbergh's connection to his characters' isolation isn't so obvious. Soderbergh returns to the notion that the characters in the first group of films—Kafka, *King of the Hill*'s Aaron, and *The Underneath*'s Michael Chambers—evoke the same sort of disconnection, but he goes little into explaining the personal reasons why he returns to such figures. Kafka's estrangement may reflect his own "feeling of disillusionment," and Aaron's detachment from his parents echoes his own, but the director consistently shies away from autobiography. In discussing *Schizopolis,* for instance, the director's only time in front of the camera—and where he cast his own ex-wife and daughter in the film—Soderbergh is willing to admit the outsider-protagonist resembles his own experience. Though the dual characters he plays—Fletcher Munson and his doppleganger Dr. Jeffrey Korchek—are wacky caricatures, the subtext of the film is deeply personal. But Soderbergh remains elusive about personal stakes, preferring to let the film speak for itself.

In the second phase of Soderbergh's career, the writer-director is even less clearly visible in his characters and his interest in their stories becomes more symbolic—even semi-political in the cases of *Erin Brockovich* and *Traffic.* Soderbergh's interest in *The Limey,* which stars Terence Stamp as a British ex-con avenging his daughter's murder, for example, comes less out of a concern with the character, per se, and more from Soderbergh's disillusionment with the present and his nostalgia for the creative energy of the 1960s. Soderbergh cast '60s iconic actors Stamp and Peter Fonda *(Easy Rider),* for this very reason, as well as including footage from Ken Loach's 1967 work *Poor Cow* in the film. "I'm interested in the '60s conceptually. I think a lot of creative people are, because it was a time of such possibility," Soderbergh explained to me in 1999. "And now, it just doesn't feel that way; it doesn't feel like the best stuff is the most popular stuff."[2] (Interestingly, it would be Soderbergh's own studio effort, *Erin Brockovich*, following a number of well-regarded Hollywood productions—e.g. *American Beauty, The Insider, Magnolia*—that would help bring the "best stuff" back into the mainstream.)

By the time Soderbergh finishes *Erin Brockovich* and begins to work on his tenth feature film, *Traffic*, a multi-part narrative about the drug wars that features several main characters, he begins to question the very idea of what makes a film "personal." In several of the later interviews, Soderbergh explains that all of his films are personal, whether or not they are strictly about his own life. "That was the real turning point for me," Soderbergh told Michael Sragow. "I wasn't interested in making films about me anymore, and my take on things. I thought, 'I've got to get out of the house!' "

Turning distinctly away from his own life and moving "out of the house"—or as he elaborated to Dennis Lim more recently, "*Schizopolis* was about detonating that house, blowing it up and putting myself in a position where I couldn't go back anymore"—Soderbergh's interest, and much of the content of the interviews, moves away from character and more to issues of craft.

One paramount technical interest for Soderbergh is editing. Soderbergh's fascination with the manipulation of time, and breaking the conventions of conventional linear storytelling is a reoccurring motif in this collection. The discussions with *Positif*'s Michel Ciment and Hubert Niogret about *King of the Hill* and *The Underneath* provide for some of the more in-depth investigations into Soderbergh's editing concerns. These discussions also keenly anticipate some of the work that Soderbergh accomplishes years later on *Out of Sight* and *The Limey*. "Our minds are totally non-linear," he tells the *Positif* editors in 1995. "It seemed interesting to try to express that in film. I had been dreaming of making a film where there would be no end to the dialogue, where the last sentence in a scene would lead to the first sentence of the next scene. It would have been like one uninterrupted conversation that

---

[2] Anthony Kaufman, "Out of Place: Dislocated with Steven Soderbergh and *The Limey, indieWIRE* October 14, 1999.

would cut across the three temporal levels, a verbal flow analogous to the interior monologue."

By the time Soderbergh gets to *The Limey*—a film he calls "*Get Carter* made by Alain Resnais"—his editing dreams have come to fruition. "I was trying to get a sense of how your mind sifts through things," Soderbergh tells Sheila Johnston in *Sight & Sound* in 1999. When I asked Soderbergh about the editing of *The Limey* later that same year, he added, "I was looking at it from the beginning as an opportunity to recreate and rewrite the movie. That was always my intention. To go and shoot a bunch of stuff and then go in and just rip it apart."

This filmmaking-on-the-fly attitude is also an ever-evolving concern for Soderbergh. Freedom—in shooting, in style, in subject matter—may be the strongest theme of Soderbergh's work as a filmmaker. He prides himself on his quick shooting method on *sex, lies* ("for most of the emotionally charged shots, we never went beyond three or four takes") and he criticizes his slow and "somnambulant" work on *The Underneath*. For his preferred working methods, Soderbergh always returns to both *Schizopolis* (as the "exhilarating" model of filmmaking of which he was most satisfied), and Lester (who championed a more open method of filmmaking, as Soderbergh says, "tossing things off, instead of being labored about what you do").

By the time I spoke with Soderbergh about *Traffic* at the end of 2000, his ideas about freedom and filmmaking had crystallized into a technique that he loosely defines as "controlled anarchy." "What you're hoping for is a series of orchestrated accidents," he explains. "It's scarier in a way, because you're not sure if something good is going to happen, but you just have to believe that the parachute will open." Soderbergh admits that this open approach is radically different from his shooting techniques when he started out. In this post–*The Underneath* phase of his career, Soderbergh prefers, for example, spontaneity and chaos with his cast, as opposed to the excessive rehearsing he undertook when he was younger. After his Best Directing Oscar for *Traffic*, Soderbergh moves into perhaps a third phase of his career, with both the career crises and box office confidence building behind him. And his goal as a director appears to be summed up with this simple desire: "to re-insert a sense of play in the films."

As Soderbergh establishes himself as a Hollywood maverick—and the comparisons shift from Woody Allen to John Huston—the concerns and career shifts indicated in these interviews provide not only a glimpse into one of America's masters of the craft, but a look at the changing world of the U.S. film industry in the late 1980s and 1990s. When *sex, lies, and videotape* was acquired by Miramax in 1989, that company was still a modest independent, coming off releases like Lizzie Borden's *Working Girls* and Errol Morris's documentary *The Thin Blue Line*. Now it is a marketing behemoth and subdivision of studio Disney. After all, Soderbergh was discovered at the U.S.A. Film Festival, a small event for domestic independent filmmakers to showcase their work. Now, of course, the festival has been renamed Sundance, multi-million dollar deals go down there each year, thousands of journalists converge to its Park City locale to catch the next big thing, and major film companies stake their livelihood on the annual January event. Commenting recently on the festival that launched his career, Soderbergh told me, "Money changes things. And that's what it became about in a way that it wasn't before. But," he continued, considering the increased economic interest in independent film, "that's inevitable."

So as the changes in independent film have evolved over the last decade, Soderbergh's role within that industry has also changed. Soderbergh credits his move to Hollywood as much to his own personal interests as to the general evolution of the film industry. "That's sort of the way the business has worked out," he told me just prior to *Traffic*'s release. "It's not surprising when you consider that the independent movement, or whatever you want to call it, has been swallowed up by the studios; so it seems inevitable that I'd be some sort of hybrid." In the late '90s and early 2000s, Soderbergh becomes an important figurehead of an industry often called Indiewood, a mixture of autonomy and individuality with the Hollywood machine's marketing and star-power. A young craftsman with a love for American movies, Soderbergh is like many of his contemporaries (Spike Lee, Gus Van Sant, Wayne Wang), in that he became swept up in Hollywood's co-option of independent film. But rather than simply use his indie roots as a stepping stone, Soderbergh and his films, while still indebted to the Hollywood system, are still very much independent, reinventing and revitalizing the forms.

"I've always had one foot in and one foot out of Hollywood," Soderbergh tells Sheila Johnston, an idea that is reiterated throughout this book. Even after his successful run with *Erin Brockovich* and *Traffic*—two films that arguably lean more toward Hollywood than independent cinema—Soderbergh's future projects reinforce his desire to retain his indie status with Hollywood access: He plans to make a sequel to *Schizopolis* and adapt Stanislaw Lem's sci-fi classic *Solaris* (already once adapted by the master Russian director Andrei Tarkovsky) which is to be produced by James Cameron *(Titanic).*

In many ways, Soderbergh's interest in straddling both Hollywood and Independents comes from a greater goal: to bring back the beloved '70s Hollywood cinema of Spielberg's *Jaws,* Scorsese's *Taxi Driver,* Coppola's *The Conversation,* Nichols's *Carnal Knowledge*—Hollywood financed, mainstream releases that broke new ground for American cinema. In Michael Sragow's interview in early 2000, the year that would bring *Erin Brockovich* and *Traffic* to the screen, Soderbergh explains his desire "to see if we can get back to that period we all liked in American cinema twenty-five years ago."

In the subsequent and final interviews, Soderbergh retains this high ambition, but with the same sort of modest approach of his early days—embodied in his famous words after winning the Palme d'Or in 1989: "It's all downhill from here." Spanning twelve more years, and as many ups as downs, the interviews in this book reveal Soderbergh to be as self-effacing and light-hearted in his later more established years as he was when just starting out. While a subtle confidence finally shows through, Soderbergh still tells Dennis Lim at the end of his most successful period in over ten years of making movies, "I was in my apprenticeship for some time and I guess I'm now finally open for business."

Per the guidelines of the Conversations with Filmmakers series, the interviews in this collection are unedited from their original publications and ordered chronologically (perhaps Soderbergh would object to the strict time line) according to when the interviews were conducted, not publication date. Though repetition is bound to occur from interview to interview, the nuances that emerge from one to the next are always unique. The first five interviews focus on *sex, lies, and videotape* alone, for instance, but each one tackles Soderbergh's splash on to the film scene from surprisingly different angles, from the irreverent, near tabloid-style exposé of *Rolling Stone* after the film's Park City premiere, to the serious interrogations of Michel Ciment and Hubert Niogret at the film's Cannes debut to Katherine Dieckmann's more psychological conversation upon the film's release in the States. I have tried in this introduction to contextualize the many themes that run through the interviews included here, but by no means is this examination exhaustive. I must give special thanks to Paula Willoquet for her excellent French translations of the *Positif* interviews, all of which are invaluable to this collection, offering the most comprehensive conversations with Soderbergh I could find; it was the only publication, for instance, that spent a good deal of time with the budding director upon the release of his under-rated *Kafka*. Also, I'd like to thank Soderbergh himself for supplying me with certain biographical facts while he was busily preparing *Ocean's 11*. And a final thanks to my wife, Ariel Rogers, whose creative contributions to everything I do cannot be measured in words, and who has helped me to—quoting Soderbergh's words—"re-insert a sense of play" in my own life.

CHRONOLOGY

1963 Born on January 14, 1963 in Atlanta, Georgia. His father is Peter Soder-
      bergh, an education professor (died February 1998); his mother is a for-
      mer parapsychologist. He is the fifth of six children. In April, the
      family moves to Austin, TX.

1967 Family moves to Pittsburgh, PA

1973 Family moves to Charlottesville, VA

1976 Family moves to Baton Rouge, LA, where his father is the Dean of
      Education at Louisiana State University and enrolls Soderbergh in an
      animation class at Louisiana State University. Frustrated with the ani-
      mation process, he uses the equipment to make Super-8 live action
      films, often collaborating with friends on their films as well.

1978 Makes *Passages,* a short film about dreams starring his younger brother
      and brother-in-law

1979 Parents separate. Makes short film *Janitor,* a homage to *Taxi Driver* and
      The Conversation.

1980 Makes the short *Skoal,* a black and white film about his impressions of
      high school. After graduating in the summer of 1980, a former instruc-
      tor hires Soderbergh as an editor in Los Angeles on an NBC game show
      called "Games People Play." Writes untitled spec screenplay about
      high school.

1981 After the show is canceled, Soderbergh works in Los Angeles in varying
      capacities, ranging from a cue-card holder, a game-show scorekeeper,
      and a freelance editor. Moves back to Baton Rouge and works at a

video arcade, giving out tokens, and makes *Rapid Eye Movement,* a short film about his time spent in Los Angeles. Writes spec screenplay *Gumshoe* (comedy).

1983   Gets a job at a video production house, shooting and editing industrial videos. Soderbergh's parents officially divorce on his twentieth birthday. Writes spec screenplay *Putting on Airs* (comedy).

1984   Introduced to the musical group, Yes. He is hired to direct a thirty-minute documentary of the band's concert tour for their album *90125.* In the fall, he is hired to shoot a concert film for Yes, to be called *9021LIVE.*

1985   *9021LIVE* is completed.

1986   *9012LIVE* nominated for a Grammy for Best Long-Form Music Video. Writes spec screenplays *Crosstalk* (family comedy), *State of Mind* (thriller set in New Orleans), and *Proof Positive* (a re-telling of *The Return of Martin Guerre* set in the U.S. during WWI).

1987   Writes *Dead from the Neck Up,* a slapstick comedy which never gets produced. In December, while moving to Los Angeles in his 1963 Buick Electra 225, Soderbergh begins formulating the idea for *sex, lies, and videotape* and writes the first draft of the screenplay in eight days.

1988   Shoots *sex, lies, and videotape* in Louisiana in thirty days.

1989   In January, *sex, lies, and videotape* world premieres at the U.S. Film Festival (Sundance) in Park City, Utah. In May, Soderbergh travels to Cannes with the film and wins the Palme d'Or. He begins planning several projects: an adaptation of *The Last Ship,* based on a novel by William Brinkley, to be executive produced by Sydney Pollack for Universal Studios; *King of the Hill,* an adaptation from A. E. Hotchner's memoir; and a film about Franz Kafka from a screenplay by Lem Dobbs. Soderbergh marries Betsy Brantley, an actress, and moves to Virginia.

1990   Nominated for an Oscar for Best Original Screenplay for *sex, lies, and videotape.* (*Dead Poet's Society* wins.) Later that year, he directs *Kafka* in Prague, starring Jeremy Irons as the Czech writer.

1991   Daughter, Sarah, is born on February 11. *Kafka* is released in December.

1992   Directs *King of the Hill* for eight weeks in St. Louis, Missouri.

1993   Directs "The Quiet Room," a thirty-minute film for a Showtime noir
       series called *Fallen Angels*. Soderbergh goes to Cannes with *King of the
       Hill*.

1994   Executive produces *Suture*. Begins production on *The Underneath*, an
       update of 1949 film, *Criss Cross*, for Universal. In October, Soderbergh
       and Betsy Brantley are divorced. Directs "Professional Man" for the
       Showtime noir series *Fallen Angels*.

1995   Produces Greg Motolla's *The Daytrippers* and writes, directs, acts, and
       shoots *Schizopolis*. Afterwards, he directs *Gray's Anatomy*, a film of Spal-
       ding Gray's monologue. He co-writes the screenplay for *Nightwatch*,
       and works on scripts for *Mimic* and an unproduced Henry Selick film
       called *Toots and the Upside Down House*.

1997   Soderbergh directs *Out of Sight* for Universal, starring George Clooney
       and Jennifer Lopez. Also produces Gary Ross's *Pleasantville*.

1998   Directs *The Limey* for Artisan. Soderbergh wins a Best Director award
       for *Out of Sight* from the National Society of Film Critics.

1999   Directs *Erin Brockovich* for Universal, starring Julia Roberts as the
       housewife turned legal crusader who helps to win a massive direct-
       action lawsuit.

2000   Soderbergh announces his involvement with a remake of *Ocean's 11*,
       to star George Clooney. After a month in release, *Erin Brockovich* breaks
       the $100 million mark at the U.S. box office in mid-April. Just a week
       before, Soderbergh begins production on *Traffic* for USA Films, starring
       Michael Douglas and Catherine Zeta-Jones, after initial deal with Fox
       Searchlight falls through. The New York Film Critics Circle awards
       Traffic Best Picture and Soderbergh Best Director. *Traffic* opens in the-
       aters on Dec. 27.

2001   Soderbergh is nominated for two Golden Globes, two Director's Guild
       awards, and two Oscars for his directing work on *Traffic* and *Erin Brock-
       ovich*. Begins shooting *Ocean's 11*. The film is scheduled for a December
       release. Wins Best Director Oscar for *Traffic*. Writes screenplay for
       Solaris to direct in the spring of 2002, to be produced by James Cam-
       eron. Announces his next film after *Ocean's 11: Full Frontal*, an "unof-
       ficial sequel to *sex, lies, and videotape*" to be produced by Miramax and
       shot in November.

FILMOGRAPHY

1986
YES 9012LIVE
Director/editor: **Steven Soderbergh**
Cast: Yes, Jon Anderson (vocals), Tony Kaye (keyboards), Trevor Rabin (guitar and vocals), Chris Squire (bass guitar and vocals), Alan White (drums).
Color, Video
67 minutes

1989
SEX, LIES, AND VIDEOTAPE
Miramax Films
Executive Producers: Nancy Tenenbaum, Morgan Mason, Nick Wechsler
Producers: John Hardy, Robert Newmyer
Director/writer/editor: **Steven Soderbergh**
Cinematography: Walt Lloyd
Music: Cliff Martinez
Art Direction: Joanne Schmidt
Cast: James Spader, Andie MacDowell, Peter Gallagher, Laura San Giacomo
Color, 35 mm
101 minutes

1991
KAFKA
Malofilm Group
Executive Producers: Barry Levinson, Paul Rassam, Mark Johnson

Producers: Harry Benn, Stuart Cornfeld
Director/editor: **Steven Soderbergh**
Written by Lem Dobbs
Cinematography: Walt Lloyd
Music: Cliff Martinez
Production Design: Gavin Bocquet
Cast: Jeremy Irons, Theresa Russell, Joel Gray, Ian Holm, Jeroen Krabbe,
Armin Mueller-Stahl, Alec Guiness,
Black and White/Color, 35 mm
100 minutes

1993
KING OF THE HILL
Universal Pictures
Executive Producers: John Hardy
Producers: Albert Berger, Barbara Maltby, Ron Yerxa
Director/editor/adaptation: **Steven Soderbergh**
Cinematography: Elliott Davis
Music: Cliff Martinez
Production Design: Gary Frutkoff
Cast: Jesse Bradford, Karen Allen, Jeroen Krabbe, Elizabeth McGovern, Spal-
ding Gray, Lisa Eichhorn, Joseph Chrest, Adrien Brody
Color, 35 mm
102 minutes

1993
"THE QUIET ROOM," *FALLEN ANGELS*
Showtime
Executive Producer: Sydney Pollack
Producers: Steve Golin, Lindsay Doran, William Horberg
Director: **Steven Soderbergh**
Cinematography: Emmanuel Lubezki
Cast: Peter Gallagher, Joe Mantegna, Vinessa Shaw, Bonnie Bedelia, Genia
Michaela

1993
SUTURE
Samuel Goldwyn
Executive Producer: **Steven Soderbergh**

Directors: Scott McGehee, David Siegel
Cinematography: Greg Gardiner
Editor: Lauren Zuckerman
Production Designer: Kelly McGehee
Cast: Dennis Haysbert, Mel Harris, Sab Shimono, Dina Merrill
Black and White
96 minutes

1994
"PROFESSIONAL MAN," *FALLEN ANGELS*
Showtime
Executive Producer: Sydney Pollack
Producers: Steve Golin, Lindsay Doran, William Horberg
Director: **Steven Soderbergh**
Cast: Peter Coyote, Brendan Fraser

1995
THE UNDERNEATH
Universal Pictures
Executive Producers: Joshua Donen, William Reid, Lionel Wigram
Producer: John Hardy
Director: **Steven Soderbergh**
Writers: Daniel Fuchs (*Criss Cross* screenplay), **Steven Soderbergh** (credited
as Sam Lowry)
Cinematography: Elliott Davis
Music: Cliff Martinez
Editor: Stan Salfas
Production Design: Howard Cummings
Cast: Peter Gallagher, Alison Elliot, Elizabeth Shue, Joe Don Baker, Paul
Dooley, William Fichtner
Color, 35 mm
99 minutes

1996
GRAY'S ANATOMY
Northern Arts Entertainment

Executive Producers: Caroline Kaplan, Jonathon Sehring, John Re, Kathleen Russo
Producer: John Hardy
Director: **Steven Soderbergh**
Writer: Spalding Gray
Cinematography: Elliott Davis
Music: Cliff Martinez
Editor: Susan Littenberg
Production Design: Adele Plauche
Cast: Spalding Gray
Color, 35 mm
80 minutes

1996
SCHIZOPOLIS
Northern Arts Entertainment
Executive Producers: John Re
Producer: John Hardy
Director: **Steven Soderbergh**
Writers: **Steven Soderbergh** (credited as Sam Lowry)
Cinematography: **Steven Soderbergh**
Editor: Sarah Flack
Cast: **Steven Soderbergh**, Betsey Brantley, David Jensen
Color, 35 mm
96 minutes

1996
THE DAYTRIPPERS
Cinepix Film Properties
Executive Producers: David Heyman, Lawrence S. Kamerman, Campbell Scott
Producer: **Steven Soderbergh**, Nancy Tenenbaum
Director: Greg Motolla
Writer: Greg Motolla
Cinematography: John Inwood
Music: Richard Martinez
Editor: Anne McCabe

Production Design: Bonnie J. Brinkley
Cast: Stanley Tucci, Hope Davis, Anne Meara, Parker Posey, Liev Shreiber
Color, 35 mm
87 minutes

1998
OUT OF SIGHT
Universal Pictures
Executive Producers: John Hardy, Barry Sonnenfeld
Producers: Danny DeVito, Michael Shamberg, Stacey Sher
Director: **Steven Soderbergh**
Writers: Scott Frank (screenplay), Elmore Leonard (novel)
Cinematography: Elliott Davis
Music: David Holmes
Editor: Anne Coates
Production Design: Gary Frutkoff
Cast: George Clooney, Jennifer Lopez, Luis Guzman, Ving Rhames, Catherine Keener, Don Cheadle, Dennis Farina, Steve Zahn
Color, 35 mm
122 minutes

1998
NIGHTWATCH
Dimension Films
Executive Producers: Bob and Harvey Weinstein
Producer: Michael Obel
Director: Ole Bornedal
Writers: **Steven Soderbergh**, Ole Bornedal
Cinematography: Dan Laustsen
Music: Joachim Holbek, Marco Beltrami
Editor: Sally Menke
Production Design: Richard Hoover
Cast: Ewan McGregor, Nick Nolte, Patricia Arquette
Color, 35 mm
101 minutes

1998
PLEASANTVILLE
New Line Cinema

Executive Producers: Michael De Luca, Mary Parent
Producers: **Steven Soderbergh**, Gary Ross, Jon Kilik
Director: Gary Ross
Writers: Gary Ross
Cinematography: John Lindley
Music: Randy Newman
Editor: William Goldenberg
Production Design: Jeannine Oppewall
Cast: Tobey Maguire, Jeff Daniels, Joan Allen, Reese Witherspoon, William
H. Macy
Color, Black and White, 35 mm
125 minutes

1999
THE LIMEY
Artisan Entertainment
Producers: John Hardy, Scott Kramer
Director: **Steven Soderbergh**
Writers: Lem Dobbs
Cinematography: Edward Lachman
Music: Cliff Martinez
Editor: Sarah Flack
Production Design: Gary Frutkoff
Cast: Terence Stamp, Peter Fonda, Luis Guzman, Leslie Ann Warren
Color, 35 mm
90 minutes

2000
ERIN BROCKOVICH
Universal Pictures
Executive Producers: John Hardy, Carlos Santos Shamberg
Producers: Danny DeVito, Michael Shamberg, Stacey Sher
Director: **Steven Soderbergh**
Writers: Susannah Grant
Cinematography: Edward Lachman
Music: Thomas Newman
Editor: Anne Coates

Production Design: Philip Messina
Cast: Julia Roberts, Albert Finney, Aaron Eckhart
Color, 35 mm
130 minutes

2000
TRAFFIC
USA Films
Executive Producers: Cameron Jones, Graham King, Andreas Klein, Mike
Newell, Richard Solomon
Producer: Laura Bickford, Marshall Herskovitz, Edward Zwick
Director: **Steven Soderbergh**
Writers: Stephen Gaghan, Simon Moore (miniseries Traffik)
Cinematography: **Steven Soderbergh** (credited as Peter Andrews)
Music: Cliff Martinez
Editor: Stephen Mirrione
Production Design: Philip Messina
Cast: Michael Douglas, Catherine Zeta-Jones, Benecio del Toro, Don
Cheadle, Luis Guzman, Dennis Quaid, Amy Irving
Color, 35 mm
147 minutes

STEVEN SODERBERGH

INTERVIEWS

Hot Phenom: Hollywood Makes a Big Deal over Steven Soderbergh's *sex, lies, and videotape*

TERRI MINSKY/1989

STEVEN SODERBEGH HAS A PILE of phone messages. Sydney Pollack's been calling for weeks. Demi Moore has invited him to lunch at the Ivy. Taylor Hackford called from his car phone. David Hoberman, the president of Walt Disney Pictures, wants to set up a meeting. So do executives at Paramount, Warner Bros., Columbia and Universal. Soderbergh sees no point in returning the call from Don Simpson and Jerry Bruckheimer, the producers of *Beverly Hills Cop*. "They're slime," he says, "just barely passing for humans."

A year ago, Soderbergh couldn't have gotten these people to look at him sideways. Then he was just some twenty-five-year-old kid come to Hollywood with six unproduced screenplays and a director's reel of fourteen-minute films he'd made in his home town of Baton Rouge, Louisiana. Now he's a twenty-six-year-old with the same reel, the same screenplays, and a $1.2 million independent feature he wrote and directed called *sex, lies, and videotape*. The overwhelming and unanimous praise this film is receiving even before it's been released has left Soderbergh stunned. It's not as if his movie is filled with big-screen moments—it has no chase scene or special effects or even, despite the title, explicit nudity. It just has four people confronting their feelings about, well, sex and lies and videotape.

When the movie was shown for the first time, in January, at the U.S. Film Festival, in Park City, Utah, Soderbergh felt the need to apologize to the audi-

From *Rolling Stone*, May 18, 1989, by Straight Arrow Publishers, Inc. 1989. All rights reserved. Reprinted by permission.

ence for his unfinished work. It was still too long, the sound mix was tempo-
rary and the titles were made on a Xerox machine. Nobody seemed to notice
or care. After the first screening, tickets to the remaining three shows became
so scarce that they were being scalped. Agents, producers, critics and even
just regular people kept stopping Soderbergh to shake his hand, to press their
cards into his palm, even to tell him that they'd seen a lot of movies but they
had never seen one quite like his. One women told him to call her if he ever,
ever needed a place to stay in Los Angeles. A man came up and asked him,
"Can my girlfriend kiss your feet?"

It's hard to know how to act when you're getting this outpouring of admi-
ration and affection. Soderbergh says he's never been very good at accepting
compliments. His first instinct was to dismiss them, as if such talk were ridiculous, but he was told that was annoying and he should cut it out. For the
week of the festival, Soderbergh could have been eating every meal courtesy
of some movie muckety-muck. Instead he took a job as a volunteer shuttle
driver.

Back in Los Angeles it was more of the same—actually, much more. The
reviews of *sex, lies, and videotape* that appeared in *Variety, The Hollywood
Reporter*, the *Los Angeles Times* and *American Film* were so laudatory that Soderbergh was embarrassed. "They're not even like I wrote them myself," he
says, "because if I wrote them myself, I would have found something to pick
at." Within a month, his agent had gotten 500 phone calls from people who
wanted to meet Soderbergh or see his movie, as well as piles of scripts and
novels for him to consider, directing or adapting. One studio offered to make
a blind deal—anything Soderbergh wanted to do.

Executives made pitches for Soderbergh to come work for them. The people at Warner Bros. said, "Look, we encourage young talent. Didn't we give
Batman to Tim Burton to direct?" The people at Paramount said, "Look, we
already do our share of big-budget extravaganzas. We need someone like you
who makes smaller, more personal films." During his meeting at Paramount,
Soderbergh found himself distracted by a bowl of fruit in the middle of the
table. He hadn't eaten lunch, and he was starving. But the bowl was filled
with bananas, navel oranges—things you'd have to peel. Soderbergh didn't
want to leave behind a pile of litter; somehow, it didn't seem appropriate
when four studio executives were comparing him to Woody Allen.

You can't let this stuff go to your head, Soderbergh keeps telling himself;
there's a term in Hollywood for what you are: flavor of the month. Which is

no guarantee of success. Far better, safer anyway, to remain suspicious and cynical of the sudden attention, to regard yourself merely as a bone that every golden retriever in town has to sniff. What about Phil Joanou, protégé of Steven Spielberg's who probably could have made any movie he wanted. He chose to do *Three O'Clock High*, which nobody saw. Soderbergh has given instructions that he be shot on sight if he ever makes a movie about high school. Or what about Michael Dinner? Soderbergh loved Dinner' *American Playhouse* production of *Miss Lonelyhearts*, but now Dinner's directing totally innocuous comedies like *Off Beat* and *Hot to Trot*. Soderbergh doesn't know Dinner, but he can't imagine this is what Dinner wanted to do with his career. Soderbergh can name a half a dozen others who have been the flavor of the month, and these days you practically have to put out an all-points bulletin to find out what they're up to.

"When you meet somebody and you haven't done anything, you're just a guy," says Soderbergh. "You know that the person's response to you is contingent wholly upon how you act and what you're like. Which is as it should be. I got to make a movie. Okay, you know? So? I'm happy that I did. I'm still a schmuck like everybody else. I have problems, just like anyone. There are people who get to make movies who are fucking assholes, who are terrible people. Okay, I know I'm not a terrible person. It's just that this attention—it's potentially harmful, and it has so little to do with sitting in a room and trying to write, trying to make something good and make something work. It has nothing to do with that."

All the same, people seem to look at him differently now, with awe; even some of his friends have started calling him "the genius"—and not sarcastically. While scores of other independent movies will go searching this year for a distributor, *sex, lies, and videotape* has eleven companies in a bidding war. Soderbergh's agent, Pat Dollard of Leading Artists, has to work until late at night just so he can give some attention to his other clients. "It's like being the manager of the Doors in 1967," says Dollard, "and their first album comes out, and 'Light My Fire' goes to Number One. It's kinda like that."

Soderbergh has to search for things to worry about, so he does. The other night he went to a screening at the Writers Guild. He hated the movie so much he walked out, but not before it registered that everybody else in the room seemed to love it. "It's scary," he says. "It was so effortlessly bad that you think that's how everything is. You begin to think, 'Maybe my stuff is like that.' " On top of that, Fawn Hall was at the screening too. Soderbergh remembers thinking, "Here's a semipublic personality out being seen, and I'm becoming a semipublic personality, and what does that mean? That someday I'm going to have my picture taken with Fawn Hall?"

Soderbergh is living every filmmaker's fantasy (including his own since he was fifteen)—that you make one picture, and Hollywood spontaneously and collectively heralds you as a major talent—and the most satisfaction he will express verbally is "Yeah, it feels nice," or "I keep expecting to get hit by a bus." A friend of his was heard asking, "Do you think maybe he's screaming inside?"

On the face of it, Soderbergh seems like the perfect, the obvious, candidate for this kind of hype. He is a movie buff's movie buff, the kind that goes to see *Altered States* eleven times in a two-week period, four of those in a single day, because the film's sound technician came to that particular theater to retune and enhance the speaker system. "I was there when the subwoofer blew out," he says, the way another person might say, "I was at Woodstock." Not only does he keep a mental list of his top ten favorite movies of all time, he also has specific rules for compiling it: "It has to be a film that if somebody says, 'Hey, let's watch whatever,' or 'Let's go see whatever,' no matter what format, no matter what time, you will drop everything and go, or sit down and watch. And it can't be a movie that came out within the past ten years, because you haven't had enough time to put it in perspective." (His ten favorite movies are, in no particular order, *Citizen Kane, The Third Man, The Conversation, The 5000 Fingers of Dr. T, The Godfather* (parts I and II), *Annie Hall, Jaws, Sunset Boulevard, The Last Picture Show* and *All the President's Men.*)

In Hollywood, where a new concept is often cast as the hybrid of two older, proven ones, Soderbergh might be described as a cross between Steven Spielberg and Woody Allen. Like Spielberg, Soderbergh had a precious interest in film and debuted as a feature-film director at the age of twenty-six; like Allen, he has made a movie that is talky and intimate and topically consumed with relationships between men and women.

Sex, lies, and videotape is about four people: John (Peter Gallagher); his wife Ann (Andie MacDowell); Ann's wild sister Cynthia (Laura San Giacomo); and Graham (James Spader), a friend of John's from college. John is having a torrid affair with Cynthia, while Ann, ignorant of their deception, finds herself increasingly disinterested in sex. The balance of this precarious triangle is tipped with the arrival of Graham. He is emotionally remote and enigmatic, given to posing the most personal inquiries as if he were making small talk. Despite the fact that Graham hasn't seen John in nine years and has never met Ann or Cynthia, he is privy to all their secrets within a few days. He is also willing to reveal his own—that he was once a pathological liar and that his disgust with himself has made him impotent, able to become excited only when watching his homemade videotapes of women talking about sex.

If anyone asks—and people usually do—where Soderbergh got the inspiration for *sex, lies, and videotape,* he tells them about his twenty-fourth year: "I was involved in a relationship with a woman in which I behaved poorly—in which I was deceptive and mentally manipulative. I got involved with a number of other women, you know, simultaneously—I was just fucking up.

"Looking back on what happened, I was very intent on getting acceptance and approval from whatever woman I happened to pick out, and then as soon as I got it, I wasn't interested anymore, and I went somewhere else. There was one point at which I was in a bar, and within a radius of about two feet there were three different women I was sleeping with. Another six months of this behavior—this went on for the better part of a year—and I would have been, bare minimum, alcoholic and, you know, going on from there, mentally screwed up.

"It was just really what I consider to be ugly behavior in the sense that it was, you know, it was lying, and it was, it was, it was sexual politics. It was manipulation; it was, it was power-tripping. It was just really bad. I just became somebody that, if I knew him, I would hate. Which was disturbing. And at the same time, I wanted to see how far I could push it."

Soderbergh put a stop to this behavior by abruptly withdrawing from all his liasons and, as an act of contrition, selling off his most-prized material possessions, his audio and video equipment. "He had the proverbial wall of sound, all that matte-black stuff, and he stripped the walls bare," says David Foil, a friend of Soderbergh's from Baton Rouge. "In my thirty-five years, I've never seen someone go through so much anguish and soul-searching." Soderbergh tried therapy but gave up after a few sessions, and now, like his movie character Graham, he regards himself as a recovering liar.

He gets different reactions to his confession, the most common being surprise. Soderbergh hardly looks like a depraved Lothario. He is six feet tall and thin, near to gangly, and considers himself unattractive. (While watching scenes of his movie, he is moved to push at the contours of his face. "Where are my cheekbones?" he asks. "Look at Jimmy and Andie—I mean, they have cheekbones. You could plane doors with my face.")

Some people, total strangers, want to engage him in philosophical discussions about their own sexual relationships. Studio executives, on the other hand, sometimes seem discomforted by his admissions. At Paramount, they just said, "Oh," and changed the subject. Maybe it sounded indiscreet to them.

Well, they asked.

When Soderbergh was thirteen, his father, a college professor, enrolled him in an animation course taught at Louisiana State University. Despite his talent for drawing, Soderbergh quickly grew bored with the amount of work required to produce just a minute's worth of cartoon, preferring instead to audit the Super-8 moviemaking class. It was his only formal film education, and the teacher's main piece of advice was this: "You can do anything you want, so long as you don't shoot footage at the zoo and then put that Simon and Garfunkel song to it."

His first completed product was an Ex-Lax commercial, starring his brother-in-law and featuring the Doobie Brothers song "It Keeps You Runnin'." At fifteen, he made a twenty-minute short, an homage to *Taxi Driver* called *Janitor*. He cannot say enough awful things about it, including, "It's just the worst thing you've ever seen." At least it had the benefit of teaching him that he didn't want to make movies about other movies, which, he says now, is the failing of most other young filmmakers.

To paraphrase Ernest Hemingway, there are two ways to make it in the movie business: gradually and suddenly. After high school, Soderbergh felt he was ready for the sudden alternative, but he had to settle for the gradual one. His former LSU instructor, who was then working in Los Angeles on the television show *Games People Play,* hired Soderbergh as an editor. But the show went off the air six months later, and Soderbergh had to take odd jobs on the fringes of the industry—as a cue-card holder, a game-show scorekeeper, a freelance editor for cable's Showtime channel.

Los Angeles, his personal mecca, now appeared to him to be the most disheartening place on earth. It was all about what you drove and what you wore and where you are. Even little things began to bug Soderbergh—like why weren't there left-turn signals on the stoplights at all the major intersections? The film schools were the worst—he disliked the pressure and the competition. There was no guarantee you'd even get to make a movie (only a handful in each class do), and if you did, it would be shown at a big public screening attended by all these Hollywood honchos. In other words, you could have a bomb even before you graduated from college.

Instead, Soderbergh returned to Baton Rouge and went to work as a coin changer in a video arcade. He also made *Rapid Eye Movement,* a comically self-effacing short about his own obsession with moving to Los Angeles and making movies.

When Soderbergh was twenty-one, an acquaintance at Showtime recommended him to members of the musical group Yes, who were looking for a young, cheap director to make a home movie for them. They liked his work so much that they hired him to chronicle the concert tour for their album *90125;* the hour-long video was ultimately nominated for a Grammy. Armed with these credentials and the draft of a screenplay, he got an agent and then a couple of assignments—one to rewrite a Disney Sunday-night movie and another to script a musical, kind of an updated *West Side Story,* for Tri-Star Pictures. It was never made.

Soderbergh wrote the screenplay for *sex, lies, and videotape* in eight days, and on half of those he was driving from Baton Rouge to Los Angeles. "It came out so fast," he says. "I just wanted it dealt with. I didn't know if anybody would read it. I didn't know if my agent would say, 'I can't send this out.' It just seemed too personal."

Soderbergh thinks of his four characters as himself cut into quarters, but it is the placid, withdrawn Graham who most apparently resembles his creator. "We never talked about it," says actor James Spader. "But there would be days when I'd get out of wardrobe and come to the set, and we'd be wearing the same thing."

The movie's development was, by Hollywood's standards, obscenely brief—it was financed (by RCA/Columbia Pictures Home Video), shot, edited and shown at the U.S. Film Festival within twelve and a half months after Soderbergh first dropped the script on his agent's desk. The snags were minor. Several talent agencies refused to show it to their clients because they thought it was pornographic. He wanted to shoot the movie in black and white, but RCA/Columbia insisted on color. And the title—which Soderbergh chose after thinking to himself, "How would Graham describe this movie?"—met with some resistance. His investors feared that potential distributors would assume from the name that it was shot on videotape instead of film stock.

"It got to the point," says Soderbergh, "where they were saying, 'You know, we can keep the first two words; *sex, lies*—that's fine. But the third word—maybe we could change the third word.' And I'm like, 'What—*sex, lies, and magnetic oxide?*' I said, 'No. You either change the whole thing or you leave it.' As long as we came up with something good. Nobody could, including myself."

The shooting, according to his actors, went so smoothly that the only issue they can recall is Soderbergh's telling MacDowell and San Giacomo to tone down their Southern accents. "We aren't doing Tennessee Williams here," he'd say. In response, they started calling him Steven Subtle-bergh.

He made $37,000 for his efforts, ten percent of which went to his agent, five percent to his lawyer and one and three-quarters percent to the Writers Guild. He owed about $5000 in back taxes, which he paid, and he bought himself a 1960 AMC Rambler for $1300. He has $2100 left to get him through the next two months of living in Los Angeles, and his monthly rent, $400, is due. Paramount, Warner Bros., Columbia and Universal have all offered to pay him to rewrite two of his scripts; Soderbergh, being conservative, guesses he could get about $100,000 to do that, but he doesn't want to be beholden to anyone.

The thing is, he could use the money. He wants to get braces. During a particularly unpleasant episode with his former girlfriend, she retaliated with a slew of withheld criticisms, including one aimed at his teeth. It was just another thing to feel self-conscious about. When Soderbergh finally makes his next movie deal, that will be the first thing he buys for himself.

Soderbergh is in an editing room in North Hollywood, working on the final details of postproduction with his friend and sound editor Larry Blake. They met nine years ago, about the time that Soderbergh was making a rather disjointed film starring the Goodyear blimp and himself doing poor Marlon Brando imitations. For that reason, it's pretty hard for Blake to connect Soderbergh with his new-found celebrity.

"I'll stand for anything," Blake says, "except for seeing your picture in 'The Great Life,' "—a column in *The Hollywood Reporter*.

Soderbergh tells him about seeing Fawn Hall at a screening. "What if somebody takes a picture," he says, "and I'm in the shot somewhere?"

"If you're in the background, then that's okay," Blake says. "But not if it's you and your arm's around Morgan Fairchild."

Soderbergh dismisses this as impossible. Still, it's certain that his next project will have a higher profile. Although he's been offered a lot of "relationship" movies, Soderbergh has a more ambitious idea for himself. He wants to make the film version of a 616-page novel by William Brinkley called *The Last Ship,* an apocalyptic epic about the men and women of a naval crew who survive World War III.

Such a project will probably cost at least twenty times what *sex, lies, and videotape* did, but he knows that he can get a deal for it, if only because Sydney Pollack has agreed to become involved. At the same time, he's embarrassed by the figures his agent is saying he's going to demand for Soderbergh's services: $250,000 to write the script, $100,000 for a rewrite, $500,000 to direct. "That's absurd," he says. "I don't want to draw attention to myself."

He's feeling guilty, too, about the distribution deal that's been made for his movie. Miramax Films had promised to pay $100,000 over the highest bid, but then Island Pictures weighed in with an extremely generous $1 million for the distribution rights, plus $1 million to be spent on advertising. The only problem was that Island expected Soderbergh and his producers to split any promotional costs above that. So they went back to Miramax and offered to wave the extra $100,000 in exchange for Miramax's picking up the tab for all the advertising. That fee, along with the $575,000 that Virgin Vision is paying for the foreign rights, meant that Soderbergh's investors will have made all their money back, and then some, by the time the movie opens in early fall.

"It's a ruthless deal, it really is," says Soderbergh. "The film has to make like $4 million just to break even." At the point the deal was made, Miramax had *Pelle the Conqueror* in release, and even though it had been nominated for two Academy Awards and had been out for nearly two months, it had just barely grossed $1 million.

Meanwhile, *sex, lies, and videotape* still isn't finished to Soderbergh's satisfaction. He's in a cutting room, excising lines from the climactic moment when Ann and Graham admit their attraction for each other. Just a few hours ago, he got his first lukewarm response to the film. Barry London, the head of marketing at Paramount, apparently wasn't impressed by it. There had been some discussion that Paramount was going to make a bid to distribute the movie, which would have been a coup, to get the promotional force of a major studio. (None of the other majors was interested because RCA/Columbia already owned the video rights, the real cash cow of the film business.)

But then Soderbergh got a call telling him that London's reaction to the movie was, "Yeah? So?"

It's exactly what he feared would happen—that the word-of-mouth has built expectations so high that people will be disappointed when they finally see it. Soderbergh has this joke; speaking in a nasal Long Island accent, he'll say, "Dawn Steel's being very cold to me," or "Ray Stark's being very cold to me." It mostly works as a joke because these people aren't being cold to him; in fact, Steel, the president of Columbia Pictures, called to tell him how much she enjoyed his movie and that she hopes he'll do something for her. And now he gets this review of his work: "Yeah? So?" Soderbergh may not want to wallow in being the flavor of the month, but he doesn't want to blow it, either; Simpson and Bruckheimer were invited to a screening of *sex, lies, and videotape* in late April.

A voice comes over the intercom into the room. "Steve! Call for you on line one." He picks up the receiver. "Hello? Yes? . . . Oh no, that was today? Oh, fuck. What time is it? . . . Ah, shit! Yeah, you better. I'll leave right now. Tell her, tell her that we just concluded negotiations, that I'm on my way . . . Yeah, it looks like the Miramax thing is . . . Yeah. Everything that we wanted . . . Everything. Yeah. Yeah. Tell them I'm running ten minutes behind."

He jumps up and then looks down at himself. Most of the time he wears what he calls his "arty, pretentious filmmaker garb"—jeans, a black T-shirt and a long black cotton coat—but today the T-shirt has been replaced by a white one bearing the words SEX, LIES, AND VIDEOTAPE.

He winces; he's forgotten that he had a three o'clock meeting at Warner Bros., and now he's going to show up for it not only late but with the name of his movie stenciled across his chest. "Oh, man," he says, "they're going to think I'm a complete dork." When it comes right down to it, he can't help wanting these people to like him.

Interview with Steven Soderbergh:
sex, lies, and videotape

MICHEL CIMENT AND HUBERT
NIOGRET/1989

Q: *What are your origins and what was your childhood like?*
A: My family moved around a lot. I was born in Atlanta, Georgia, on January 14, 1963 and after living in a number of different places we finally settled down in Louisiana when I was thirteen years old. My father was an education professor and he would change jobs whenever he was offered a better position elsewhere. He would let me see any films I wanted. As a result, when I was ten or eleven, I discovered films like *Five Easy Pieces, The Conversation, Scarecrow* that had a tremendous impact on me. When I was thirteen, my father was teaching at Louisiana State University in Baton Rouge and there was an animation course taught by film students to adolescents. Knowing that I was interested in cinema, my father signed me up for the course; but it soon became too draining because animation is laborious work. So I got a camera and started shooting live action and I discovered that this was an ideal form of expression for me, through words and images. I could use all the equipment from the course and needed only to provide the film stock, and I ended up making a number of shorts.

Q: *In what genre?*
A: During the first phase, as is to be expected, I mimicked the films I liked. So, when I was fifteen, I made an homage to *Taxi Driver* on Super-8, a film that fascinated me. It was so bad and everyone around me was so negative about it, that I had to rethink everything and conclude that it was not such

---

From *Positif,* September 1989. Translation by Paula Willoquet. Reprinted by permission.

a hot idea to make films based on other films. At that time, I had also seen Fellini's *8½* and I discovered that a film could be an expression of one's personal point of view. So I decided that that was the direction in which I wanted to go. The films I made after that were more direct; they reflected my mental and emotional states. They were experimental and impressionistic, but at the same time they had a quasi-documentary feel in relation to myself, and only lightly manipulated reality.

Q: *How many shorts did you make?*
A: From the time I started making films until about two years ago I think I made six or seven shorts, about twenty minutes each.

Q: *Did you have other interests besides film when you were young?*
A: Besides books, not really, because I was totally absorbed by making films even at the expense of my studies. It was not until 3 or 4 years ago that I started getting interested in other forms of arts, like theater, dance, music, because I realized that I needed to enlarge my horizons. But reading was always necessary to me. When I was about fifteen and my films were becoming more experimental, I was very drawn to Faulkner because of the interior monologue and the way he allowed disparate emotions and ideas to flow from one another. At that time, when I was shooting, I had a pretty casual attitude toward tight narratives. I wanted to capture mental states. The last short I made in high school is still one of my best, in terms of technique and content. When I saw it again six months ago I was expecting a huge gap between what I was doing at seventeen and what I do now, at twenty-six, and I did not really notice a gap. The title was *Skol!,* which means "Cheers," and also it was the name of a very popular brand of tobacco among high school students. It was a film about my impressions of school and my thoughts, a series of vignettes shot in black and white. I benefited from some lucky accidents: one exchange we shot in slow motion during a football game was in perfect synchrony with a piece of music from Glenn Miller's "Moonlight Serenade." My father had written four books on big band music so I was very familiar with Tommy Dorsey and Glenn Miller.

Q: *Since you spent much of your childhood in the South, do you feel any bonds to that part of the country?*

A : Probably. All kinds of strange things can happen in the South. It's also culturally a very rich part of the United States. Even if its history is not always very positive, it is fascinating. Frankly, I saw more racism in the North than in the South, and Boston, for example, is the most racist city I know. Maybe because the rhythm of life is slower, I always felt that the South was more conducive to writing and thinking.

Q : *What did you do after you made* Skol!*?*
A : I was a Senior in high school in 1980 and I was seventeen. After graduating, I liked the idea of going to Los Angeles and I had pictured a life for myself very much like the one I have had in the last four months! My luck was that my professor at Louisiana State University—where I had audited classes while I was in high school—had left that summer to work for NBC in Los Angeles. I got in touch with him when I arrived and he suggested that I work with him editing some short documentaries he was making for television. One was about a team of deaf football players from Colorado; the other was about a juggling competition. They were about 7 or 8 minutes long each and were shot on film and transferred to video to be edited. I continued working like that, including for *sex, lies, and videotape,* because it's a lot faster, and people like Kubrick also started working like this. In 1980, people thought that was strange, unusual. It was a great experience for me; I had the opportunity to work in my area and to see my work appear on the screen. After six months, in 1981, they canceled the program. I did all kinds of odd jobs for the rest of the year so I could pay the rent—I counted points during televised games, for example—but it was very depressing. Los Angeles quickly started feeling like the worst place on earth, where people were judged based only on their material success. So, I went back to Baton Rouge feeling like a failure and with little hope for a future in filmmaking. I got a job that paid 66 dollars a week in a video arcade, where I gave out coins to people to put in the machines. The arcade was near the university campus and my father—who had split up with my mother while I was still in high school—would come to see me in the evenings and would encourage me when I was embarrassed to be doing something a monkey could have done. All the while, I continued to read and write and started to work on a film, bit by bit, for the next 16 months. It was called *Rapid Eye Movement,* a kind of impressionistic vision of my let downs in Los Angeles. It was a cathartic experience for me; the expression of a mental process, and for that reason the

film underwent many transformations from conception, to execution, to the final product. These changes took place progressively as the film developed— which in some cases can be a negative thing, but in this case it was not and *Rapid Eye Movement* is one of my most satisfying shorts. But, like the earlier shorts, it was made for my friends and me; I was not showing it to anybody else. In early 1983, I got a job with a video production firm where I worked in production and post-production. I shot and edited industrial films for about 2 years. During this period, I also spent time in Los Angeles where my friend had asked me to come help him edit some programs. Toward the end of 1984, he got a call from a collaborator of the rock group, Yes, who was looking for an inexpensive director to make a film about their tour. That's how I found myself on the road for 10 days and brought back a documentary. Since I was not paid very much, I adopted a pretty irreverent attitude and this 30 minute film was a lot like the first films of Richard Lester. Mostly, I wanted to have fun without worrying too much about how they would react, but finally they did rather like my work. They weren't happy with my video editing so they sent me to London to redo it, then they suggested I work as an intermediary between the band and another director who had been commissioned to shoot one of their concerts. I turned them down because this annoyed me and went back to Louisiana. Two months later, they finally asked me to shoot their concert. I was 21, had never filmed a live show, and in the Fall of 1984 I found myself in Canada with 8 Panaflex cameras shooting 2 evenings of concert. All went well and I finished editing the film, *9012Live*, during the Summer of 1985. I remember sitting in their offices lamenting that I could not shoot a script I had written. They told me to find an agent. Which I did. I had her read my script, showed her *Rapid Eye Movement* and a piece of the concert film, and she liked them. She started representing me and got me several small jobs as a scriptwriter.

Q: *What was your script about?*
A: Again, it was very personal and set in Baton Rouge. In many ways, it was a first version of *sex, lies, and videotape*. It dealt with the relationship between men and women, with the absence of communication and with misunderstandings. But in spite of many rewritings, I could not make the script work. I think I was still caught in a very adolescent way of thinking and had never really had a profound relationship with a woman, which would have enabled me to cast a more mature look at the relationship between the sexes.

Q : *Had you written other scripts?*
A : Yes, but they weren't any good. One was about relationships inside a high school and the other was a detective story treated as comedy. I knew they were not successful, but it was good practice.

Q : *Aside from the contemporary films you already mentioned, which filmmakers were you most attracted to?*
A : Certainly, people like Orson Welles and Howard Hawks. And also comedy directors like Preston Sturges and Lubitsch who made a big impression on me. Some of Wyler's film too, and *Sunset Boulevard*, and *The Third Man*. Mostly, American films. But, of course, I was also influenced by works like *Rules of the Game*, *The Bicycle Thief* or *Diabolique*. Strangely enough, I know very little of Bergman—I don't think I saw more than 3 of his films, even though my paternal grandfather was born in Stockholm. But I saw the films in a chaotic way, because of the availability. I also experienced the changes that occurred in American cinema of the mid '70s as a devolution—with the arrival of blockbusters at the expense of the mature works of the new American cinema who had impressed me so much, Rafelson, Scorsese, or Coppola.

Q : *Did having an agent change the way you operated?*
A : I continued to write personal scripts fairly quickly so she could evaluate each one. I was also able to work on 2 commissioned works. I wrote a television script for Disney, which was never shot, and a musical comedy for TriStar, which was never shot either. With the money I received from TriStar I shot my last short, *Winston*. That also was a version of *sex, lies, and videotape*, the story of a woman who creates an imaginary life for herself so she can keep a man who was after her at a distance. To a certain extent, it was inspired by things that were really happening in my life, but this made the whole project problematic. When I saw the film a year later, I realized I had not been objective enough for it to work. But it was an important experience, in particular because of my work with the actors. The style—camera placement and movement—was also close to what I used in *sex, lies, and videotape*. When I was finishing the film, early 1987, my life was a lot like that of the husband in *sex, lies, and videotape*. . . . It was a real problem for me because I was beginning to feel very unhappy and I had to put an end to my behavior and begin thinking about the effects it was having on other people. I was living with someone I really liked but at the same time I was behaving miser-

ably and I wanted to know why. So I sold everything I had, except my books, put some belongings in a car and decided to give Los Angeles another shot. This was at the end of 1987, and a few days before leaving I started to write a first draft of *sex, lies, and videotape,* which I continued to work on during my trip to California. When I arrived in Los Angeles, I gave it to my agent, not knowing what she would think because this had been for me both an act of liberation and remorse. She liked it a lot and the positive reaction on the part of the producers was pretty immediate, to the extent that this was a film about sexuality, with four young and attractive characters, which could be made for just about one million dollars, which is not a great risk. So much so that between the time I put the script on my agent's desk and the premiere of the film at the U.S. Film Festival, only 12 months had gone by.

Q: *How many versions of the script did you write and what were the changes you made?*

A: I wrote three versions and the differences are mostly in the tone. The structure stayed the same except that in the first version there was no resolution at the end: Ann and Glenn had very little contact with each other. She goes back into therapy, Glenn leaves the city, the husband is not scarred by the experience, and the sister disappears. Nobody finds a way out. This left me dissatisfied because I wanted a feeling of movement. The first version was harsher; it gave mostly an impression of anger. But the more I distanced myself from the events that lead me to write the script, the more I became capable of making the necessary adjustments. Then, during the rehearsal week with the actors, preceding the shooting, I rewrote some of the dialogue so it would fit each actor. The scenes were not changed from a content standpoint, but I wanted to be sure that each line of the dialogue was connected to what the scene was expressing, that each explored the sub-text as much as possible, and the actors really helped me on this. I encouraged them to add what seemed natural to them. The shooting went smoothly in 30 days. I always had the impression that we had lots of time and I never came to the set with a list of shots. It was when the actors were playing the scene that I would decide on camera placement. The most takes we did were eleven, and that was because of technical problems. But for most of the emotionally charged shots we never went beyond 3 or 4 takes. We had a lot of fun, you know.

Q: *What were the rehearsals with the actors prior to shooting like?*

A : For one week, we read the entire script 3 or 4 times with all the actors. And for the rest of the week I worked on each scene with the actors in pairs. We incorporated some of their improvisations and that's when their characters took on a definitive form. What I wanted was to create an atmosphere of experimentation where all inhibitions disappeared, because I knew I was going to ask a lot from them and it was important that they feel at ease. I really believe in casting. Once you have picked the person who best suits the role, I think you have to let them play the part without giving them too many directions. When we started shooting there was mutual respect. They had read the script and had felt it deeply. As for me, I had seen their previous work and had appreciated it a lot. During the shooting they were free to make mistakes, which is very important. As for the rhythm of the film, it established itself from the outset. What strikes me when I watch contemporary American films is their impatience. I don't know if it's because the filmmakers are not sure of themselves in relation to their subject, but in any event, they give the spectator no breathing space, they don't allow the spectators themselves to establish the connections among the scenes. I wanted a natural rhythm, because when I talk to people in real life, conversations last more than two minutes; not everything that is said is of the greatest importance, and every other sentence is not a joke. I have tried to reflect back the kinds of human interactions, of verbal exchanges that I have experienced myself. The actors were relaxed because we had a small crew and in Louisiana, where we shot, none of the producers were there. It was really just us.

Q : *When you are shooting a small budget film like this, with only four actors, your choice for the first actor must surely influence your choice for the others, to the extent that you are playing with oppositions and contrasts.*
A : That's exactly right. While I was casting, I saw a bunch of actors that I liked and in my mind I was imagining different groupings of four people. The first person I cast was Andie MacDowell, by pure coincidence. I had seen her in *Greystoke* and *St. Elmo's Fire,* but I wasn't aware of the breadth of her talent. When one of my executive producers told me she wanted to audition, I was not particularly interested. I thought she was beautiful, and I knew she was a model, but that's all. But when she came for her screen test, I was blown away. Then I went looking for someone who would be aesthetically different, with black hair for example. Soon after that I saw Laura San Giacomo. She was sensual and attractive, so she could seduce any man she

wanted; but at the same time, because she wasn't as beautiful, one could understand that she would be intimidated by her sister's looks. So, after choosing the females, who were both in their thirties, I had to find the men. I had a hard time for Graham. I went to Los Angeles and was told that James Spader was interested in the role, which surprised me because he usually plays characters that are rather unlikeable. But he was great in his audition and he convinced me. He then suggested I talk to Peter Gallagher, whom he had just met. I thought he would be a good contrast. They got along well in real life, but at the same time they had very different working styles, which served their antagonistic relationship in the film well. It was Gallagher, who had a lot of stage experience playing roles from writers like O'Neill, who had to bring the most to his character because the husband was the least well-defined character in the script.

Q: *Is this because of your personal experience?*
A: Maybe, although in theory, at that point in my life I was closer to the James Spader character. I think it was mostly because I was too harsh toward the husband, who was just a sketch. In treating him like that I was punishing myself for what had happened. What Peter brought to the role was humor, a diabolical charm. You can see he is a seducer, while in the script he was just a jerk.

Q: *Did you come up with the title right away?*
A: When I finished the script, I did not know what I was going to call it. I asked myself how someone like Graham, direct and honest, would describe the film. And I thought about these three words, which by the way seem to me to summarize all the themes of the film, which are also the themes of modern America: the selling of sex, the practice of telling lies, and the invasion by the video. We were afraid that the public—what we thought would be a limited public—would be turned off by this title which suggested surveillance. In any event, the audience over forty could find it sordid. But we thought that once they had seen the film they would not have this impression, and that through word of mouth this message would get around. The first screenings worked out just like that. The publicity and the reviews would also confirm that this was not an exploitative film.

Q: *Did you plan in the script the specific uses you made of video.*

A: Yes. We scripted every moment we went in and out of video. It was necessary, if nothing else to protect myself. For me, the video was a useful strategy
to give one of the characters a certain distance in relation to the others, and
to enable him to maintain it until the end. This is also in keeping with the
prevalent role of video today in American society. Someone told me that the
video plays more or less the same role played by letters in the 18th century,
which makes sense to me.

Q: *The film progressively shifts from an ironic to a more serious tone.*
A: From the beginning, I knew the story would become increasingly darker.
But I think that in the last part there is still some humor. The barometer for
me is Graham's comment: "Do I have a problem? I look around me and
when I see Cynthia, John, and me, I feel pretty good." In general, the audience laughs at this point because it's a very strange comment. The first third
is lighter because there are many exposition scenes and you are getting to
know the characters, who at times are funny without intending to be. But
this progression toward a darker tone was intended on my part and the person in charge of casting called after she had read thirty pages of the script to
tell me how funny it was. I told her to call me back once she had finished
reading the script. One hour later, her state of mind was not the same! If I
changed the ending in a more positive direction it was not out of compromise. My personal experience has taught me that after periods of torment
and suffering, there comes a healing process where you learn that the hard-
ships you have had taught you something. And this is what I wanted to show
in all honesty. Besides, many American independent films are depressing at
the end in order to prove that they are not "commercial" and I did not want
to fall into that trap. I wanted the film to be what it needed to be, and not
the result of a position taken in relation to other considerations. To sum up,
this film came from the gut. And for me the end is ambiguous: I don't have
a clear sense of what's going to happen to Graham and Ann. Nor to the other
two characters. I am not sure that John is going to lose his job. For me he
represents a certain type of American for whom what is bad is not to do
something reprehensible, but to get caught. It happens everyday in American politics.

Q: *If your film is very American in the way that the characters talk about themselves, the way you use language and the role you give conversations also makes*

one think of films like The Decline of the American Empire *or of those of Rohmer, Bertrand Blier or Bergman.*

A : I am going to seem ignorant to you. I am not familiar with Denys Arcand's film, and I still need to discover Rohmer and Blier! Based on what I've been told, there must be connections; but since I'm in Cannes I am embarrassed that I have not seen them. On the other hand, I like Wim Wenders' work a lot. I saw *Wings of Desire* many times; I like its slow rhythm and its emotion. The only unpleasant thing about this festival is that he is the head of the jury committee and since I am competing I can't talk to him. I'll have to write him a letter when this is all done.

Q : *Your rhythm is similar to that of certain American films from the early '70s, like those of Rafelson.*

A : Certainly. And also to a film like *The Conversation.* Kubrick too is not in a hurry in *Lolita.* When you trust your material, you can take your time, but you can't fall into the trap of complacency.

Q : *The film crew, were they about your age?*

A : For the most part. Walt Lloyd, my director of photography, is in his forties, and he is the only one I brought from Los Angeles. All the others are from Louisiana and had worked with me before. Walt is not only a remarkable artist, but also someone whom I like very much. His cinematographic style in this film is seductive but discreet; it never calls attention to itself. Walt is also someone who is very sensitive toward the actors and he sets his own shots. This is important because the actor expresses an emotion along a certain line and my job is to follow this line closely. Walt knew what was the best angle to capture this emotion. I am well versed in the technique and I can plunge myself into it, but the only conversation I had with Walt about it led to the decision not to use a telephoto lens. If we wanted to be close to the characters, we would simply bring the camera close to the actors, even if that made them feel that the lens was physically too close to them. We did not want, however, to fill the screen with their faces, let alone the eyes. There too, the Hollywood classics offer an example. You can count on one hand the number of extreme close ups in a Hawks film.

Another important contribution was Cliff Martinez's music—he's in his thirties. I wanted it to be discreet and to reinforce the atmosphere. Without the music, the last scene with Ann and Graham on the couch would not have had the same emotional force.

Q : *What are your future projects?*
A : I have five or six scripts already written. But I am not satisfied with some of them. I have two immediate projects. One is an adaptation of one of William Brinkley's novels, *The Last Ship*. It's once again a story about men and women, sexual tensions, but on a larger scale and in extreme situations. I have just signed a contract with Universal and I was able to convince Sidney Pollack to be my executive producer, which makes me feel more secure in my dealings with the studio. My other project is to work on two other scripts. One of them, *The Mistaken Theory*, is a verbal comedy, with a fast rhythm in the style of Preston Sturges. The other, *State of Mind*, is a thriller set in New Orleans. They have taken the place of the two older projects: *Dead from the Neck Up*, a slapstick comedy written in 1986 which I have put aside for the time being because a film which is too similar, *Naked Gun* was just released in the U.S., and *Revolver* which I started writing at the end of 1987 and which I put aside in order to work on *sex, lies, and videotape*.

Q : *How was the production of* sex, lies, and, videotape *set up?*
A : I had several producers who played crucial roles at different times. Nancy Tenenbaum negotiated single-handedly the universal rights with Virgin by simply showing them the script and her enthusiasm. They had never seen any of my previous work and had never talked to me on the phone before fronting the money. Robert Newmyer, one of my producers, closed the deal with RCA-Columbia Home Video for the American distribution. As for John Hardy, he set the budget with me at 1.2 million dollars and was physically the producer during the shooting in Baton Rouge. I suppose this film reflected my desire to return to the scene of my childhood, rather than to choose a big metropolis like New York or Chicago as the setting. I wanted it to be the middle of the country.

Steven Soderbergh, King of Cannes: Truth or Consequences

HARLAN JACOBSON/1989

"I always think that everyone else is having a really good time, and I'm not having anywhere near as good a time as they are."—Steven Soderbergh, in Cannes, before winning the Palme d'Or

"Now I think that everyone else thinks I'm the one having this really great time and resent me for it."—after winning the Palme d'Or

FEDERICO FELLINI, *La Dolce Vita*, 1960; Luis Buñuel, *Viridiana*, 1961; Luchino Visconti, *The Leopard*, 1963, and *Death in Venice*, 1971; Michelangelo Antonioni, *Blow-Up*, 1967; Robert Altman, *M*A*S*H*, 1970. And so on and so forth goes the parade of winners of the Palme d'Or at Cannes, the crossroads of cinema aspiration and art, right on down through Coppola, Scorsese, the Tavianis, Olmi, Schlöndorff, Kurosawa, Wajda, Wenders and Steven Soderbergh, *sex, lies, and videotape*, 1989.

Soderbergh?

Originally slotted to screen in the Directors Fortnight, the post-'68 sidebar event meant to house the upstart kids outside the main competition, Steven Soderbergh's *sex, lies, and videotape* not only ended up in competition, it staggered Cannes by stealing three top prizes: Best Film, Best Actor for James Spader and the international critics' prize.

It was Soderbergh's first film, and at 26 he is Cannes' youngest winner of the Palme d'Or. And yes, he came from Nowhere (Baton Rouge, La.), and the

From *Film Comment*, July/August 1989. Reprinted with permission of the author.

film cost Nothing ($1.2 million). And the buzz has moved from the inside of his head out into the world.

Past Palme winners have been swept away in the blue sea of May to wherever heroes dine in Elysian fields, not to be seen again save for the next day's page one photos. Not Soderbergh. He hung out in the Majestic bar after the ceremony, looking like he was trying not to have the good time the sore losers were sure he was having. Gandhi swept ants out of his path; Soderbergh apologizes to water for drinking it.

The next day he made the obligatory trek to the Colombe d'Or restaurant out of town (Yipes, grownups!), but that night there he was having pizza in a sidewalk cafe with a Miramax vice-president who had confidence to spare and a honeymoon couple he didn't even know and who looked like they'd only just met at the wedding. They'd have choked on their crust if only they'd seen what Soderbergh does to young marrieds in the most stunning update from the Sex Wars front since Mike Nichols' weighed in with *Carnal Knowledge* two decades ago.

In that film, Nichols drew and quartered the male psyche—the project was limited to investigating the limited emotional development of the educated, upper-middle class American male. On the one hand was Art Garfunkel's simpering worship of child-women; on the other, Jack Nicholson's fire-breathing, rampart-battering assault on the trusting hearts of one Rapunzel after another. Sixties men—meaning college boys—shuddered for their futures: the choice was either down on their knees to virgins, or paying witch doctors to dance the hard dance.

Soderbergh arrives on the scene 20 years later to choreograph two men—and two women. Each pair starts out on different ends of the continuum that runs between appetite and hibernation, between the truthful self and the deceitful, between power and paralysis, between sex and love. Moreover, since Nichols' time the Invisible Woman has died: what women accept in lieu of intimacy is as important here as what men do to avoid it.

The matched pair of scenes I liked best involve frigid wife Andie MacDowell, slipping upstairs in the middle of the night to observe the sleeping form of her husband's long-lost college friend, James Spader, precisely as she comes to realize he has awakened something sleeping inside her; and her rising from bed to confront husband Peter Gallagher with her fears he's having an affair with her sister, Laura San Giacomo, whose voice sinks about three octaves lower than legal and makes the blood run hot.

sex, lies, and videotape sees the frontier of filmmaking not in the stars or the sequels but in the small European and sometime American independent traditions of investigating the way we love each other, or fail to. There's no room for space cowboys here; nice guys finish with busted lips but whole beings.

There are hits and misses in the film—the character of the husband seems more an idea of a depersonalized twit rather than the complicated force that might attract one woman to the altar and her sister to bed. No dinner could survive a husband saying about his wife, "Usually, Annie achieves a critical mass with the salt . . ." Their mismatch is too apparent, and so the dice seem too loaded with dynamite to warrant surprise when the explosion comes in the third act.

But if Soderbergh has knit the film together too tightly at times with lines of dialogue that set up the next move or visual signs that echo—in the pivotal moment the wife shows up in the same black t-shirt and blue jeans favored by the friend—he has tried very hard to be very real. He has showed us our skin, how it wants to be touched with truth and beauty and eternity, and the consequences of that time called our twenties. That is to say, it is about the end of the first time, and the beginning of wisdom. *sex, lies, and videotape* is not Bertolucci's *Last Tango in Paris*, which mixed myth with the lure of redemption, but then what is?

Perhaps what disarmed the jury in Cannes, chaired by Wim Wenders—whose own masterpiece, *Wings of Desire,* is a hymn to the reunion of men and women, of the two Germanies, of the past and the present—wasn't simply Soderbergh's mapping out a small square of the terrain. But, like Wenders, he too wished aloud that in the end we find each other and heal.

Your film is about the way people leave each other, the way they escape or drive each other away. Is this drawn from personal experience?
Yeah, I guess so. I drove the most important woman in my life to leave because I didn't want to be in the relationship but couldn't cop to it. I'm still trying to figure why I couldn't just say, "I don't want to be in this. I want to be out of it." There was nothing wrong with the person that made my life uncomfortable. I just wasn't ready to deal with the responsibility. So I was very deceptive about how I got out of it. And then once I was out of it I couldn't even allow it the dignity to die properly. I kept stringing it out and not letting it go and then I got involved with some other people and—it was just a mess. I look back on it and I'm stunned that I had turned into the kind of person I despise.

In the film I tried not to be judgmental. However you act, accept the consequences. I don't have control over how other people act. And I don't like movies where a relationship, which has a lot of grey areas, is presented definitively as bad. If you're dealing with a cop movie, maybe you need to have some definite delineations. But then again, maybe not.

Were there certain movies that served as guideposts?
No, not really. There were two problems when we were trying to get the film off the ground. One was that it didn't synopsize well. And there were no references I could make to other films in that classic Hollywood shorthand to bring an image to somebody's mind. I really didn't know how to describe it. There were films that I grew up with—*The Last Picture Show* or *Five Easy Pieces*—about relationships, but they were about different things.

It was interesting to see the male and female psyche put up onscreen and watch you chart the way for a meeting ground. There is a kind of movement in it . . .
I'm a big believer in movement, any kind of movement, as long as you feel as though you're moving somewhere. There have been times in my life where the movement turned out to be backward but I needed movement. When we talk about women leaving men more often, maybe it's just a realization that they don't have to settle any more. I don't know how right it is for you to ask someone to change for you. You've either got to say, "Fine, I can live with you," or you've got to get out.

I approach relationships now with a longer view than I used to. I didn't used to have a view at all. Each day it seemed to just spring into full bloom that day. And now I slow down—I used to get involved really fast. You know, sex clouds everything. It's hard to be objective when a physical relationship is pleasing. I've been very conscious of keeping sex out of the early stages, and I'm convinced this is something substantial. It hasn't really worked yet.

The film is, up to last August, the sum total of what I've been able to put together and figure out.

After we finished the film I went to New York to reestablish contact with somebody—the relationship that led me to write *sex, lies . . .* And it was good, we were able to be friends. We went to see *Italian-American Reconciliation* [written and directed] by John Patrick Shanley. The people were all compulsively verbal and emotional. That's very Italian. By comparison my film seems so repressed. It's all about people who will not say what they're thinking unless they're really pushed into a corner and poked. I realized how much I was like the film, how much I'm still struggling with the distance I feel between myself and other people, and my feelings, and how difficult it still is for me to feel and not instantly analyze.

What did you think would happen to you if you told lies?
Pardon me? What do you mean? When I told them what did I think?

Why do you think you began lying in the first place?
I don't know. The lies were specific only to my personal relationships with women. If I'd been able to conduct my personal life the way I conduct my professional life, I'd be in great shape, because I'm very straightforward professionally.

I can theorize for days about how I was lying to the people that I was involved with. Part of the larger problem has to do with my relationship, or lack of a relationship, with my mother, who is a great lady, a nice lady, I just don't have a relationship with her. It's just not there.

I was very intent on getting acceptance and approval. And then once I got it, I went somewhere else and got it. I'd think, "Gee, if I can get such and such to like me, then I must be okay. I must be attractive. I must be dynamic." And, of course, once you hooked her you'd look for somebody else. It just fed itself.

And then I compounded it with stupid, romantic notions of self-destruction. The starving artist phase is bullshit. You know, it is not fun. At some level, I was interested in how low can I go, how far is this going to go? And then I realized it could go on indefinitely. I looked for the bottom and realized there wasn't one. It was just a spiral until I either dropped dead or got hit by a car. That's what really woke me up. And I put a very cold and abrupt stop to all of it.

How'd you do it?
I confessed to everyone and quit having contact with anybody. Gradually, when I started feeling a little bit better, piece by piece I reestablished contact. I was sorry I had hurt them and put them through a difficult situation that I was trying to fix in private. It's taken a long time.

Did you do this on your own?
Yeah. I had earlier tried to go into therapy and it was a mess. I lied to my therapist. I went to three sessions and walked in one day and said, "Look,

I've got a handle on this. I'm making real progress and I feel really good
about myself." I mean, I just lied my ass off. And he only charged me for 15
minutes. He said, "That sounds great."

Was this down in Baton Rouge?
Yeah. Maybe the therapists aren't good down there. I can't hold him responsible, I lied to him constantly. How could he help me?

Maybe he knew anyway.
I hope so, for his sake.

It sort of becomes a game. Did you think the women ever knew you were lying?
Yeah, one of them did. The most important one did. But, boy I was wriggling,
I was wriggling. I could backpedal like you wouldn't believe.

Why'd you start?
I had great parents. My parents are divorced but it was not an ugly thing. I
had a very good upbringing. Yet appearances were important and things
were sublimated to maintain a certain image.

I told everybody what I thought they wanted to hear. It was never consistent because everyone wanted something different. It got to a point where I
thought this doesn't work. It's stupid that one organism consisting of ten
zillion cells thinks it can relate to another organism that has ten zillion cells.
But that was just in a particularly dark period and now I understand how it
can work.

How were you able to get somebody to believe that this could be a picture?
Well, on the one hand it may seem like a risk. On the other, remember that
we've got four relatively young people drenched in sexuality in a film that
can be made for $1.2 million. It was a risk only because we had no domestic
theatrical distributor and the video was already owned, which is the big
thing that you entice a distributor with.

How did you get it going?
It was Bob Newmyer's at Outlaw Productions contact at RCA-Columbia
Home Video that got that deal happening. And Nancy Tenenbaum negoti-
ated the deal with Overseas Entertainment. The script was pretty much there,

and John Hardy of Baton Rouge was going to produce it. I'd taken the script first to Nick Wechsler. Nick took it to Musifilm, but they dropped out. It was Bob who thought maybe I had something that more than ten people would see. His tastes are very commercial and mainstream in a good way. When he asked to read the script, I said, "Bob, it's not that you're stupid, it's just not your kind of movie." He read it and said, "I couldn't put it down. I had to find out what was going to happen."

How did you know that women get up in the middle of the night and watch us while we sleep?
I don't know. Even when I was being a pinhead I still had my ears open. I'm pretty observant by nature.

Tell me a little bit about video and why you used it as a metaphor for distance.
Video is a way of distancing ourselves from people and events. We tend to think that we can experience things because we watched them on tape. For Graham [Spader] this was an aspect of myself taken to an extreme measure. He needs the distance to feel free to react without anybody watching, which, I guess, is the definition of voyeurism, even though I think voyeurism has mostly negative connotations. I guess it should. I don't know.

That's show biz.
Well, yeah, I guess I always think of Michael Powell's *Peeping Tom* [1960]. . . .

Yeah, but sometimes Spader had the annoying moral superiority of a priest at confession.
I never thought of it that way. Only because I had a complete lack of religious upbringing. My parents were both lapsed Catholics and so I grew up believing whatever I wanted to believe.

Did you live with your mother once they divorced? Or your father? Did you go back and forth?
Well, kind of. My parents physically separated when I was 16, and when I was 17 I graduated high school, so I left to go to Los Angeles for a while and I eventually came back but lived outside the house.

What made you want to be a filmmaker?
I had seen a lot of films as a child. My dad would let me see anything.

What does he do?
He's a professor of education at LSU. And he enrolled me when I was 13 in an animation class. I could draw really well but it immediately became apparent that it was too much work for too little result. I made two things that were six seconds long and said, "This is bullshit." And so I just started shooting.

I'd take the camera off the copy stand and go shoot live action and I was good. I had four years of access to equipment doing all phases of everything with no pressure. I feel bad for these people in film schools who get chosen to make a film. In L.A. they have their projects screened in front of the industry. Your career could be over before you're a junior in college.

I learned at 15 that I can't make films about other films. And after making a couple that people actively hated, I learned by trial and error to make things that are more personal. Now the stakes are so high you can't learn. Super-8 was a great format. I'm sorry it's gone. I made things technically every bit as good as *sex, lies. . . .* when I was in high school.

Did you rehearse a lot on sex, lies?
We rehearsed for a week before we shot and I rewrote dialogue. I tried to make sure that I didn't let the camera dictate the performance. I'd walk on the set, we'd block the scene, and then I'd decide the camera angles. Figuring out where to put the camera is just insanely easy—if you watch, it becomes self-evident. To do it the other way around seems really stupid.

You hire the best possible people and you let them perform. I tried to help. Most of the time they were doing things better than I could ever have thought. There were a couple of times where I'd just shut everything down and the actor and I would sit there for a half an hour and talk it through until we were both comfortable about what had to happen and why. I don't know that I'll be able to do that on the next film.

Some people say, "Gee, I want to know more about why they're the way they are." I kept their backgrounds to a minimum because there's a whole other film there.

When John (Peter Gallagher) sits down and watches the videotape of his wife, what does he see?
You should ask Peter. John was the least well drawn of all the characters, and he was unafraid to look terribly unsympathetic. He came up with a lot of stuff—the plant bit, etc.

Why did you lowercase the title?
It just looked better. I looked at it in capital letters and it looked wrong. Also, I have two commas in it. I'm with the Chicago Manual of Style on that one.

It really just looked better?
It does aesthetically.

It wasn't e.e. cummings?
No, I just thought aesthetically it looked better. That's all I care about, how things look.

But that's not in the Chicago Manual.
What lowercase? They probably specifically rule against it. But I can go either way on the comma thing, and in this case I want two commas.

So is Cannes scary or fun or what?
It is so weird. I can't explain to you how weird it is.

Are you scared?
I don't know. It was beginning to dawn on me this afternoon: Denys Arcand has a film here, Bertrand Blier, Spike Lee, who I like a lot. And then I flipped through the program and there was our page with my name and, you know, it was in French. I began to really shake.

It feels like it's more exciting happening to somebody else than me. I feel like Spike Lee's having a much better time. I feel like it must be much more exciting to be Spike.

Why do you think that other people are having more fun?
I always feel like other people are having more fun wherever I am. Especially at parties. Maybe they are. It's like the Stephen Crane story about the paranoid poker player, thinks he's being cheated. He gets into an argument with another guy, and the guy shoots him dead. And then we find out that he was being cheated. But the point of view is that the guy has completely lost it. And so now I have the fear that everybody else is having more fun than me. Maybe I'll be at a party someday and accidentally back into the room where everybody is having a great time.

Well, everybody needs to be mirrored and told that they did good stuff.
Too much of it's harmful. I realized I could just do the festival circuit for the next 8 months. You walk in, they treat you like royalty and everything you say—to your face anyway—is taken very seriously. And that's horrible. It's like being a rock star. That's why I'm trying to get out of L.A. quickly.

Where are you going to go?
To Virginia. Charlottesville. Louisiana is going down the toilet at an amazing speed and I just can't go back and live there anymore. I have time to think. I want to adapt and direct this novel that we set up at Universal.

What's it called?
The Last Ship by William Brinkley. It is sexual tension taken to an extreme you can't imagine. It's about men and women on a Naval destroyer that survives World War III. Once they find some place habitable, they start over again. But since there are three times as many men as women, the women have all the control and draw up a plan for how this is going to work. After *sex, lies* . . . I thought, "Where do I go with this subject now?"

Reading *The Last Ship* was great. It's perfect material for me to do, I thought. And so Bob Newmyer at Outlaw bought the book last year and was on the verge of signing to do it as a mini-series. And I said, "Give me four weeks to get a big producer attached."

I met with Sydney Pollack, who had seen *sex, lies* . . . and he agreed to be executive producer. He pitched it to Universal—it was like playing with Michael Jordan, and you're the rookie. You give Michael Jordan the ball and he dunks it. You know, I walked into the room, I said ten words, Pollack pitched for 15 minutes. The guy goes, "Great, let's do it." And we leave. And that was it.

Do the men survive?
Yes, they do. Although the American men are sterile, as we find out. They've been irradiated. But a Russian sub shows up at this island and they've been underwater the whole time, so they can. . . .

They're pretty fertile.
Yeah, and they haven't seen women in a long time.

Candid Camera: *sex, lies, and videotape* Director Faces Reality

GENE SISKEL/1989

THE WORLD-BEATER IS WEARING RUMPLED WHITE jeans and a white T-shirt and looks more like a movie usher than a world-class director.

"The airline lost my luggage," explains Steven Soderbergh, who, at 26, stunned the movie world in May by winning the prestigious Palm d'Or, the top prize, at this year's Cannes Film Festival for writing, directing and editing his first dramatic feature film.

In the sports world, that is the equivalent of a rookie pitcher throwing a perfect game in the World Series—except that Soderbergh's achievement took a lot longer.

Soderbergh was in Chicago recently to promote his film, *sex, lies, and videotape,* the story of four people's lives as revealed by their sexual actions or inaction. It opens Friday at the Water Tower Theatre.

"I look at the film, at the four characters, as my own personality cut up into quarters," Soderbergh says. "At times, I've acted very much like the husband [who is having a torrid affair with his wife's sister]. Other times, I've been in the Graham mode [the husband's impotent friend, who relates to women sexually only by videotaping them talking about their sex lives]. I've also been like Cynthia [sleeping with her sister's husband] when there was a political content to my relationships with women. And there are times when I've been like Ann [the frigid wife], feeling very prudish and put off from

sexual things." The film is the story of how Graham, the videotaper, enters
the others' lives and liberates them and himself.

Rare is the American filmmaker today who is so candid about sex without
making anything even approaching a porno film.

"What is ironic," Soderbergh continues, "is that this is a culture obsessed
with sex, but only up to a point. In the movies, for example, they're more
than willing to show a representation of the sex act, but I don't think a lot
of films want to deal with the real responsibilities and implications and
repercussions of sex.

"There are incredible emotions leading up to and following the physical
act of sex. And that's what I wanted to concern myself with; not with the act
itself, which I think doesn't vary that much for any one individual."

How did Soderbergh arrive at his sexpertise? How many people has he
slept with? "That's the first time I've been asked that question," says the
director. "More than two and less than, uh, 15.

"But I think I owe any insights I may have to my upbringing. My parents
offered to tell me anything I wanted to know about sex, but I never asked
them. More importantly, I was encouraged to discuss or pursue any issue that
came to mind. And ultimately, I became fascinated with how we become
defined by our views on sexuality. It really determines how I relate to other
people.

"Soon after I meet someone, I wonder what kind of relationships they
have: Are they the dominant person? I usually construct a whole story about
their private life, and I typically find out I'm wrong after I get to know them
better."

Soderbergh got to know that he loved making films after his father, a professor of education at LSU in Baton Rouge, signed him up, as a teenager, for
a class about making animated films. "I was a pretty obsessive kid with a lot
of energy. At 14, when I got my hands on a camera, I found the outlet I was
looking for.

"Film is a great medium if you are obsessive-compulsive. You can indulge
yourself in both the technical and aesthetic areas. I got into directing quite
naturally because, when I started making little films, there was no one else
to help me. Editing is the most exciting process, because that's where what
you can do with the medium becomes most apparent."

Soderbergh says his talent was apparent in his first short films, beginning
in high school. "I've probably made six finished short films, ranging from 15

to 20 minutes in length. They're all semi-dramatic narratives. And typically they are pretty accurate representations of my state of mind when I made them.

"For example, in my last year in high school, I shot a scene of a pep rally in extreme slow motion with Glenn Miller's 'Moonlight Serenade' playing over it. The rally was something that I felt compelled to be a part of but I felt very distanced from, hence the slow motion. The song? My father had written four books on big bands; it just seemed to fit."

After high school, Soderbergh ventured to Los Angeles for 18 months, working as a free-lance editor. He returned home to Baton Rouge to write scripts, occasionally flying out to Hollywood to edit for Showtime. That led to his being introduced to the rock group YES, which asked him to direct its feature-length concert movie, *9012LIVE*.

That film led him to an agent and to an independent production company willing to stake him to develop what would become *sex, lies, and videotape*.

"The quality of my early films is virtually the same as *sex, lies, and videotape*," Soderbergh says. "You could splice together my last three short films in front of 'sex, lies,' and you wouldn't notice any difference in quality. I'm amazed at what I was able to do in high school. It makes me think I should be further along now."

Soderbergh isn't bragging. Rather, he seems to be obsessed with telling the truth, with removing the mystery from whatever it is he is talking about—be it sex or film.

"With filmmaking, a lot of people have this impression that it's magic," he says. "It's not. It's a process that requires a lot of work, continually refined by a great number of people."

He speaks in a quiet, methodical manner, not unlike the character of Graham, the videotaper, as played by James Spader.

Sex, lies, and videotape was made for only $1.2 million, about one-twentieth the cost of the average summer sequel. The film features a camera that slowly tracks its four characters as they talk to each other, lie to each other, have or avoid sex with each other and try to confront themselves on videotape.

"I used the tracking shots," Soderbergh says, "because I knew that I had a very talky film and I didn't want it to be visually static. Without detracting from the performances, I wanted to keep things moving. I also wanted a very predatory feel, the idea of encircling a character and getting closer. It seemed

to fit a sort of languid quality that I wanted to have and that Baton
Rouge—my hometown and the location of the movie—seems to have.

"The three films that I kept in mind while making *sex, lies* were *The Last
Picture Show, Five Easy Pieces* and *Carnal Knowledge*. They all were made in
1971 and have a very honest quality, much different than films today."

One might expect that, flush with his Cannes prize, Soderbergh already
would have purchased a home in Hollywood, perhaps even have bought into
the Southern California life-style.

No way.

"I'm living in Charlottesville, Va.," he says. "It's a small college town,
home of the University of Virginia. I was living in Baton Rouge, but I decided
I wanted to move. I lived in Charlottesville when I was a kid and my father
was teaching there. It's very beautiful, quiet, and seems very far away from
L.A."

Soderbergh clearly enjoys keeping his distance from Hollywood, both
physically and in terms of the reality-based movies he likes to make.

"With *sex, lies*, I was making something that I wanted to see. There is an
irrational fear in Hollywood that people go to movies to escape—that they
don't want to see reality. There are certainly times when I think that's true,
but I think there's an equal appeal to escaping into somebody else's reality.
For me, it's the same thrill of hearing about somebody else's life. I have a
keen interest in that.

"The sad fact is that a film that is among my Top 10 favorite movies of all
time is really what started the trend away from reality and toward the block-
buster thing. It's *Jaws* [1975], and I love it, but it lowered the target audience
for movies as soon as Hollywood saw all the money they could make that
way."

Predictably but refreshingly, Soderbergh has no interest in filming a sequel
to *sex, lies*, even though we could easily speculate about what will happen to
the characters in the future. "I can't imagine what will happen to them,"
Soderbergh adds. "This script is all that I had to say about those four people."

Next on tap for him is a film of the novel *The Last Ship*, about male and
female sailors in conflict on a destroyer. While sex is not a prominent theme
in the futuristic story, Soderbergh allows that the Russian sailors turn out to
be potent, whereas the Americans are not.

Liar, Liar, Pants on Fire: Steven Soderbergh Comes Clean

KATHERINE DIECKMANN/1989

CHARLOTTESVILLE, VIRGINIA

The cashier at Little John's New York Deli (possibly Little John himself) is telling Steve Soderbergh about the behavioral quirks of Jessica Lange, who has a farm outside of town. Soderbergh is privy to this unsolicited monologue because, a few days back, he met a *Newsday* photographer in this restaurant, and the cashier recognizes the 26-year-old director as a contender for latest local hero. Soderbergh moved from L.A. to this genteel college town to get away from a world where "everybody wants to know me" (and to return to a place he remembers fondly from his junior high school years, when his nomadic family landed here.) But just a week after his arrival, the media seems to have ferreted him out already.

Despite his urge for privacy, Soderbergh pays polite attention to the deli man. (The director's the kind of guy who, the previous night, resisted chewing out a waitress about the hairs in his hash browns; instead, he arranged the strands on the table murmuring, "I dunno, I kind of like them all together.") Soderbergh nods his head, which rests on an inordinately straight neck, lending him an alert quality. After all, he does like to listen—he's on a constant, low-key cruise for incidents.

But, so are journalists. Over at our lunch table, I've just opened the Sunday *New York Times*. There, in the Arts & Leisure section, is a sizable feature on Soderbergh and his Palme d'Or-winning debut feature, *sex, lies, and videotape*, a modest and unnervingly accurate study of deception and healing between

From *Village Voice*, August 8, 1989. Reprinted with permission of the author.

the sexes. "Hmmmm," I note, "front page." "But below the fold. Pretty bogus," Soderbergh returns. (That could sound arrogant. Or glib. Really, he's joking.) His copy of the *Times* sits on the next table, unopened; he's already seen the piece, as well as a lengthy *Film Comment* interview that arrived a couple of days back by fax. Until his boxes come, the fax machine is one of the few objects in his rented house—that and a futon, some books, a Beatles tray with loose change on it, framed posters of *Blue Velvet* and *Brazil* lying on their sides, and one of those see-through Polaroid cameras.

While I read the *Times*, Soderbergh flips through the current *Rolling Stones*, perusing an Axl Rose interview I've recommended for its mind-blowing stupidity. "Basically, this guy is the male equivalent of a skag," he concurs. Soderbergh too, has been interviewed by *Rolling Stone*—a controversial piece in which he called the powerful producers Don Simpson and Jerry Bruckheimer "slime, just barely passing for humans." That article also contained ripe details about just how much *sex, lies* derives from a period in Soderbergh's life when he drank too much, philandered, fabricated, and blew a major relationship. The confessionals were one thing—in part a logical extension of his postlying ethnic of unconditional truthfulness (he peppers his speech with "frankly" and "to be honest."). But he was mortified by his mean-spirited attack on the moguls. So he wrote a letter to the magazine, recanting, and went to the producers' office to apologize in person.

"They just wanted to know why I would say that without even knowing them, how I formed that opinion," Soderbergh says, a little pained, admitting he based it on a piece he read in *Esquire*. "But now, from all the interviews I've done, I know that everything is always written from a slant, a particular point of view. Also, I learned that it's unfair to pass judgment on people in a forum where they have no opportunity to respond." He halts for a moment. "And that I should never say anything unless I can stand to see it blown up in a gigantic caption."

Those potentially humiliating pull-quotes and Soderbergh's quizzical, bespectacled face have been vying with *Batman,* Spike Lee, and Dennis Quaid in this summer's hype wars. All the attention detracts from the fact that his astringent mea culpa is quite direct and surprisingly simple. *Sex, lies* is about a smug lawyer named John (Peter Gallagher), who's having an affair with the slinky sister (Laura San Giacomo) of his beautiful but repressed wife, Ann (Andie MacDowell). John plays racquetball and sneaks out of the office for quickies, while Ann keeps up the good housekeeping and visits the shrink.

("It's closet misogyny," Soderbergh says of the couple's set-up, "and very Republican.") When an old college friend of John's drifts into town, the triangle bends to accommodate a problematic fourth side. Graham (James Spader) is muted, mysterious, ascetic. He lost his true love by lying to her. Now impotent, he relates to women by asking them to reveal their sexual histories and preferences to his Handycam. And, like some docile, unprurient Ugly George, he gets his subjects to open up. Then, alone, he watches their bashful talking heads, doubly detached from experience.

Although there are some superficial similarities between Soderbergh's life and the film's story, it's tough to pinpoint how this wise, competent piece came into being. Soderbergh started making Super-8 shorts as a teen in Baton Rouge, Louisiana, where *sex, lies* was shot, then skipped college to move to L.A. and work in the industry. He learned to scriptwrite and edit hands-on (with its canny blend of image and voiceover, the editing is an essential component of *sex, lies*). After cutting a music video for Yes, the group asked him to make a rockumentary; in 1986, the movie, called *9012LIVE,* won a Grammy. Soderbergh says the script for *sex, lies* "just sprang from my head" while he was driving cross-country in January 1988. He wrote a first draft over the course of a week. Six months later, he shot the film on a budget of $1.2 million (most of it from RCA/Columbia Pictures Home Video). However, when it was first completed, people weren't exactly knocked out.

"Frankly, the producers and friends who'd worked on it had a reaction of 'Well, it's okay,' " Soderbergh offers without rancor. "Nobody said, 'I think you've made a great film.' It was like, 'We haven't embarrassed ourselves—and it's still too long." But when it debuted at the U.S.A. Film Festival in Park City, an untrimmed *sex, lies* (it's now eight minutes shorter) won the Audience Award, critics spouted nearly unequivocal praise, and the deal-making phone calls began. Then came the top honor at Cannes—plus a Best Actor award for Spader and the international critics' prize.

The success of *sex, lies, and videotape* stems in part from the movie's pleasing construction. Soderbergh says, "When I was writing, or even making the film, I didn't see anything larger or wider than a face and a little bit of space around it" (which pretty much describes Graham's videotapes of women as well). It also represents a significant tonal shift from the coy irony of most current American cinema (the Coen Brothers, Susan Seidelman, and other members of the kitsch school); there's no easy cynicism. With a literate script and full-bodied performances, *sex, lies* is closer in spirit to certain late-'60's and early-'70's pictures—*Five Easy Pieces, The Last Picture Show, Carnal Knowledge, Chinatown.* Those movies resonate because of their powerful revelations about lust and love, and Soderbergh saw them at a highly impressionable age. He still reveres them for their "maturity and control."

It's telling that "maturity" (along with truthfulness) is of prime value to Soderbergh, for what's really remarkable about his movie is its more or less seamless emotional sophistication. The depiction of sibling rivalry is dead-on without being blatant, and if Graham seems to embody the tired concept of the (male) outsider-as-savior, Soderbergh's female characters are ultimately the more powerful ones, the true aggressors—they wind up controlling situations with both libido and mind. "As far as women are concerned, and there's no real rhyme or reason, but I'm certainly drawn to people who I feel are strong and don't need to complete their lives," Soderbergh explains, and adds that most of his girlfriends have been quite a bit older than he. "I had to resist the impulse to get too deeply into the two sisters in *sex, lies* because it was a whole other movie that really interested me."

Most people in their twenties, especially men, aren't all that analytical yet about their dealings with the opposite sex. "Oh, I don't know," Soderbergh continues, and then drawing on the fact that he's only a year and a half younger than I, asks, "When did *you* start looking at your love life and seeing repetitious patterns?" Ok, but that doesn't mean I could *articulate* them. Well, Soderbergh adds, neither could he, at least not at first. Early drafts of *sex, lies* were largely unresolved and full of "inward-aimed anger." The characters of Graham and Ann never even made contact, and John's infidelities went unpunished. "It was kind of 'and so it goes,' " Soderbergh says. However, in the first cut, the film's complex centerpiece—a protracted exchange between Graham and Ann in which he makes a videotape of her until she, frustrated, turns the tables—was originally far more decisive. As it stands now, the confrontation ends in a hesitant kiss and a switching off of Graham's camera, which encourages viewers to imagine an off-screen tryst.

"In the early version of the film it was very, very clear that they didn't have sex," Soderbergh says. "And in a stunning reversal, Bob Newmeyer, one of my producers, suggested I make some cuts to make it less obvious whether or not something happened. Sometimes I still don't know if we even went far enough." (Actually, he may have gone too far. The latter parts of the movie are over-explanatory, and don't make good on the film's initial ambiguity and pervasive anxiety.) "But it's been my experience that after going through immense pain and suffering, there's a time of healing and moving forward. It's also been my experience that what goes around, comes around." Ah, the theory of karmic comeuppance. Such is the fate of the self-congratulatory lawyer, John, who not only gets caught, but also jeopardizes his most prized possession, his job. John is by far Soderbergh's least dimensional creation; he's a cartoonish jab at careerism (as opposed to Graham's vindication of bohemian values). Soderbergh protests that he "never thought of John as representing anything but himself." Then he adds, "Except he's the guy who's gotten away with everything his whole life, and certainly I think his attitude typifies that of the American government, which is that the only crime is getting caught."

So does Soderbergh hate John? "Well, at a certain point in my life I *was* that character, in the sense that I was deceptive and manipulative. I didn't want there to be anything charming about him." The scene that most completely points up the parallel to the director's chronic lying phase ("I mean verbatim") is the one where a sleepless Ann wakes John and accuses him of being unfaithful. Scared, he pulls a *Gaslight* on her, inferring she's suffering from her own hysteria. "I've had men come up to me and say, 'That scene was my worst nightmare,' " says Soderbergh. "And I was tempted to say, 'Why, it's happened to you?' Someone told me about a woman in a screening who, during that scene, kept hitting the armrest and muttering, 'Yes! Yes! Yes!' "

But if Soderbergh likes to ally himself, superficially at least, with John, the parallels between the director and the character of Graham are far more provocative (and obvious). For one thing, Soderbergh's speech patterns can sound a hell of a lot like James Spader's Graham. When I mention the similarity, Soderbergh demurs, "Jimmy kinda talks like that, to be honest"—though if you look at the actor's previous, lockjawed performances (in *Wall Street, Baby Boom, Less Than Zero*), there's none of that "patented stutter-pause thing," as Soderbergh calls it. Both live like bullimics: binge and purge. Once, for instance, Soderbergh sold all his personal possessions, save his books. When CDs became available, he promptly traded in his vinyl, because, he says winkingly, "I strive for clarity in everything." And in a journey not unlike Graham's, Soderbergh drove from California to Charlottesville, alone, in his 1960 Rambler (with his Palme d'Or, cheesy-looking and already falling apart in the trunk); it could just as well be Soderbergh talking when Graham praises the "cleanliness" of living in his car because then he needs just one key.

Above all, like Graham, Soderbergh believes in direct questioning as a tonic for falsehood. When he discusses the various interviewers he's encountered over the past few months, he says, "I feel like I got to know them as well as they know me." He has opinions on all of them—this one was really smart, this one was sloppy with the facts, this one invited him to his kid's birthday party, this one rearranged information to make him sound bratty. But he trusted them with honest answers, delivered the autobiographical goods, even when it seemed risky. "Frankly, so much of it is a tacit agreement, and I can't keep saying, 'This is off-the record.' " But he does expect a little return—an "I'll show you mine if you show me yours" attitude.

Thus, when Soderbergh and I are having beers Saturday night in a near-empty bar, a tinny Fleetwood Mac medley in the background, he shifts abruptly out of a discussion about making videos—"my mind just doesn't work that way, and it's not something I want to do"—by inquiring, "So. Are you in a relationship?" (Contrary to appearance this is not a come-on. Soderbergh is currently happily involved, although the details of that relationship are something he does not want discussed.) To a certain extent, his mind just works disjunctively, as when he sums up the bad period in his life by commenting, "Ultimately, you can only stack up all the reasons, and it doesn't add up to an event, an action. Oh, this is 'Tusk,' With the USC marching band. Why? But the song works."

I tell Soderbergh what he wants to know, but in retrospect, I wish I'd reminded him that interviews are, at their best, a little bit like therapy. One person—allegedly neutral—is there for the express purpose of extracting information from the other. Normally, profiling a stranger is not about making friends, or about mutual true confessions—though of course there's no such thing as neutrality, and lines do get crossed. Then again, Soderbergh mistrusts therapy (which fits). "To me, a therapist is a paid friend, but the problem is, I don't know anything about the therapist, and I know my friends. For all I know, the guy could be saying things like, 'Steve, I think it would really help you to get a pet, and then later I found out he's, like, fucking animals or something."

It comes out that Soderbergh was in therapy for only three sessions. I tell him that's probably not long enough to make a judgment. "But it was so obviously wrong for me." Therapy or the therapist? "Both." Why was therapy wrong? "It just . . . it did . . . I wasn't ready, y'know. I mean, if you can't . . . I just wasn't ready. I don't know, I guess I have some Christian Science thing where I think, 'Oh, I can fix it.' "

Soderbergh tells me about a scene he cut from *sex, lies* where Ann, after getting closer to Graham, goes to her shrink (played with cool acerbity by Ron Vawter) to tell him she wants to stop their sessions. "He starts by saying, 'Ann, in life there are hidden agendas, and you have to understand that Graham may have his own motives for not wanting you to be in therapy.' He puts her in a kind of trance. Finally she agrees to continue with it, and he says, 'Do you think we still have progress to make?' and she says, 'Yes.' And he says, 'That's good, because I think so, too.' And she says, 'But you don't have ulterior motives for saying that, right?' And he goes"—Soderbergh mimics a demonic chuckle—" 'Heh Heh heh heh.' It just makes you want to take a shower."

One of the points of *sex, lies, and videotape* is that all this quacking about feelings can be a method of stalling the truth rather than getting at it. Certainly that's the case with Graham, who, for all his sincere posturing, doesn't ever seem to learn anything from his videotaping that would help him break his celibate torpor. ("Up until the end, I don't think he sees anyone as a person," Soderbergh offers. Everybody knows someone who tells them everything but reveals nothing, who uses "honesty" as a shield. And honesty, too, can be disarming, a form of putting someone on the spot, and thus another kind of manipulation. I tell Soderbergh that one of the strongest moments in the movie is when Cynthia, the randy sister, talks to Graham's camera about her sexual past; describing the first time she jerked a guy off. She says, "Then I started moving my hand, and then he stopped talking." That silence has its own power—and it's not necessarily sexual.

I ask Soderbergh how he went about writing Graham's character, how he concocted a figure who could get women to speak frankly about a very personal topic. "I was guessing," he says. Later, he adds, "But there are specific things he wants to know, and for his subjects to digress is a waste of time." We pause for a moment. I'm remembering the Fleetwood Mac medley in the bar, the song Soderbergh and I shared a chuckle over, because its video version has the band members lip-synching in a barn. The song bounces catchily along, the harmonies syrupy-sweet. "Tell me lies, tell me sweet little lies. . . ."

An Exploration of the Work *Kafka*

MICHEL CIMENT AND HUBERT NIOGRET/1992

Q : *At the end of our last interview, after the screening of* sex, lies, and videotape, *you mentioned two projects and two other scripts that you had decided not to shoot. None of these four projects was* Kafka. *What led you to make this second film?*
A : Indeed, at the time I thought that *The Lost Ship* and *King of the Hill* would be my next films and that *Kafka*, about which I was already thinking, would come next. I gave up on *The Lost Ship* after writing a first version because I couldn't find a solution for the third part. The book, on which the script was based, did not follow a chronological order and when I laid out the story for the cinema, it did not work. So I told Sydney Pollack and Universal that I wanted to put *The Lost Ship* aside for a while and make *Kafka* right away. Finally, I completely abandoned *The Lost Ship* because developments in the international situation rendered it obsolete. People today no longer worry about nuclear holocaust, even if in two years they start thinking about it again. It was a huge project and I had too many doubts to pursue it.

Q : *How did you become aware of the script for* Kafka?
A : In 1985, my first agent—she died in a car accident in 1988 and her younger brother took her place—gave me a script from Lem Dobbs as an example, and at the time I wanted to learn to write a script. I loved Dobbs' work, but I did not think that someone someday could make a film of it. I was afraid that those who would be able to raise the money for it would not appreciate its potential. Nevertheless, the first version contained many autobiographi-

From *Positif,* April 1992. Translated by Paula Willoquet. Reprinted by permission.

cal details that I decided to exclude. There were many scenes with the father, Anna, the fiancée, etc. Today, many people complain that the film is neither a biography nor an imaginative work, which is exactly what I did not like about the first version of the script. I wanted to stick to the thriller and, in a way, Kafka was the protagonist only by accident. So, I started cutting things out and we went from 140 pages to 110. Most of the scenes that were cut were family scenes.

Q : *In what way did Lem Dobbs' script seem like a model of narrative technique to you and your agent?*
A : He is a writer who knows how to suggest images without having to give directions for camera angles, etc. He is an excellent writer, very powerful, whose technical knowledge is rare in the U.S. nowadays. I now have in my possession all of Lem's original scripts, and they are great. Only one was shot, *Hider in the House,* but it was rewritten by someone else during the scriptwriters' strike. Now, he is getting ready to shoot his first film based on one of his scripts, *Edward Ford,* a fascinating work which I would have liked to make. It's about Midwest character, a kind of Travis Bickle [the hero in *Taxi Driver*], who is obsessed with B films and who goes to Hollywood at the end of the '50s to become an actor in this kind of film, without realizing that it does not exist anymore. We follow him for 25 years while he tries to get a card from the Screen Writers' Guild. It's the funniest and the darkest piece of Americana that I have read in a long time.

Q : *How did you work with Lem Dobbs?*
A : It was a rather complicated relationship, and when the film came out, we had a public run in, of sorts. He reproached me for having changed his script, which was not entirely true. At the beginning, we worked closely together on the changes. He was present when we started shooting, then he left. There are a number of scenes on which I worked alone, especially those with Jeremy Irons and Theresa Russell. When I showed the first cut to friends, it became clear that the film was not working, that there were problems particularly with the scenes that I had rewritten myself. Lem's "voice" was very distinct and I was not able to recapture his tone. There were also scenes written by him that were not working either. Lem had seen the first cut and he thought it was a train wreck! So I drew up a list of all the scenes that did not work and I asked him to rework them, to help me. Which he did. I really

think that the film today, in its final form, is better than anything that ever existed on paper. Maybe Lem wouldn't agree, but that's what I think. This was a situation where you had two reasonably intelligent people, with very definite ideas about cinema, who often agreed, and sometimes didn't. We talked every week, we planned to work together, he is a very intelligent person and I like him a lot. It seems natural to me that over a two-year period we would have some arguments. What happened is that, unfortunately, a journalist from the *New York Times* met Lem the day after Jeremy Irons had said in an interview that the story was not as successful as the visual aspect of the film! This made Lem mad, and the journalist chose not to publish the favorable things Lem had to say—because Lem liked the film, without loving it—and only reported on his dissatisfaction! One shouldn't exaggerate the significance of this incident because we are still planning on working together on another project. He simply felt that at times I was being arbitrary and I felt that he was sometimes difficult. But he also knows that, in the final analyses, as the director, I'll do what I want, just as he will when it's his turn to be behind the camera. I did not find him overly dogmatic, and maybe he is simply more demanding that I am.

Q : *Did you shoot some scenes in London?*
A : They were interior scenes. When we decided in February 1991 to shoot certain scenes, we knew, because of the schedules of some of the actors, that we had to start filming on May 1 for 10 days. We were not going to shoot in Prague and since these were studio interior scenes—in the café, in Edouard Raban's apartment—we went to Pinewood. We also reshot all the scenes where you don't see the microscope, in the color sequences in the castle. I did not like what was happening with the first version of the film, nor the visual aspect. We had found these huge hallways, 100 meters long, in the building of the military archives of Prague, but unfortunately you couldn't control the light. All the planes were equally lit and I did not have the various planes of light that I wanted. So I had to reconstruct the whole thing in the studio and this gave me the opportunity, at the same time, to change the unfolding of events inside the castle. The introduction of Doctor Murnau, for example, is very different from what it was initially. Originally, we simply had him come into the office. In the new version, Ian Holm has the freedom to go from A to B, to go from the image of a servant to that of the boss.

Q: *For your second film, you could have shot a comedy of interior emotions like* *sex, lies, and videotape, which would have made you an auteur figure in the eyes* *of the critics. You chose, rather, to make a radically different film.*

A: I know that some people had imagined an entire career for me because of *sex, lies, and videotape.* According to them, I should have shot a certain type of film, but I knew I wouldn't. So I thought that I might as well disappoint them right away by making something completely different but which, at the same time, corresponded to what I had been wanting to do for a long time since. As I told you, I had read *Kafka* three years before making *sex, lies, and videotape.*

Q: *Did Kafka, the writer himself, interest you as subject for a film?*

A: I would have never thought about it before reading the script. I thought a biography of Kafka would be boring. As for Kafka's books, they have certain faults as cinema material, as is evident in the cinematic adaptations I've seen. His works are grounded more on ideas than on events, which does not really work for the screen. As fascinating as Orson Welles' *The Trial* is, it shows its limits. As a reader, of course, I feel differently and am very interested in his themes. I thought the connection that Lem Dobbs established between Kafka and expressionism was pertinent, and that Doctor Murnau was a logical development of these ideas. His script seemed to escape all the traps of a biography and of an adaptation, while keeping all that seemed interesting to me: the foreshadowing of Nazism by twenty years; the bureaucratic thinking leading up to the Third Reich, etc.

Q: *The character also reflected your own preoccupations.*

A: My two films have in common a protagonist who is alienated and disoriented, bewildered by the world around him. Kafka hides behind his camera and the hero of *sex, lies, and videotape* hides behind a camera! Both films are about digging in order to find a hidden truth. This also attracted me. You have to understand that I made my first film very comfortably, shooting a small film in my hometown, without witnesses. So I wanted then to go in a different direction and do something difficult, uncomfortable. I could afford it because things were going my way. I knew that making my second film was like crossing a street knowing that in any case a car was going to run over me. As it is, I chose to cross at the busiest intersection. Nonetheless, I was not able to foresee the possessive attitude toward Kafka of certain American critics. That an American would consider Kafka an icon seems a bit strange to me. This film mixes so many ideas and genres that the reaction would be to consider it either an utter failure, or a success that was difficult to attain. I have to admit that it was the first attitude that predominated.

Q: *Unlike in your first film, here you had to recreate a world that you have not known.*
A: In reading Kafka's biographies, as well as his works, his correspondence, his diary, I found many affinities with his way of thinking. When you go to Prague, it all falls into place. When you read Kafka before knowing Prague, it's as if one out of every six words was missing. But while walking around town, each of his words starts to fill in the gaps. I could not stress enough that there is something intangible that permeates everything in this city. I can't explain why, but it's a very mysterious place. At first, the city does not reveal herself to you easily, it's a very slow process. When I was scouting out locations, I realized that Prague would become a character in the film. After that, it was not difficult to keep that in mind. Every day we were confronted with strange experiences. If nothing else, because of our dealings with the Barrandov studio. For example, everyday we had to ask for electricity on a particular set. One day, we had no electricity! We checked that we had in fact filled out the forms, and they told us that we had not requested that the guy who turns on the electricity be there. We were right in our subject matter. I tried not to behave too much like an amateur in the way I shot Prague, and when I see the film I feel the city comes across well on the screen.

Q: *When did you decide to shoot in black and white and to later use color for the sequences in the castle?*
A: Everyone who read the script had no doubts about it: the film had to be made in black and white. Lem wrote it from this perspective. There were references to German expressionism all over the place. On the other hand, there were many debates about the use of color. One day, Lem told me in passing that Stuart Cornfeld, one of my producers, thought of using color because the castle made him think of Oz, the magician's town. I liked the idea of opening the door and, all of a sudden, allow the foundation that had been established during the first 77 minutes to crumble at our feet, given the feeling that something was going to happen. Nowadays, the convention for using black and white is to reference a dream, a fantasy, the unreal. I liked

the idea that in this case it would be the opposite. The more I thought about it the more I thought that certain story elements would be more forcefully expressed in color, like the idea of the microscope, of the brain and the eye. We did a test in black and white and it did not work as well. As a whole, the film expresses an intensified reality so it seemed to me we had to go a step further in entering the castle. For this part I wanted a colorful range, strange, disquieting, and uncomfortable. The black and white photography offered us some challenges. The film stock has not changed in 30 years; it is not very sensitive. The image is grainy. The stock contains a lot of silver nitrate and it catches static electricity in an unpredictable way. We couldn't do anything about it, and we had to reshoot a number of scenes. The negative is very vulnerable between the time it is shot and the time it is developed. I imagine that when all films were in black and white, labs had ways to avoid this kind of accident, but today it's a lost practice.

Q: *Did you show Walt Lloyd, your cinematographer, old black and white films which might inspire him?*
A: In fact, we gave him a long list and he did not know most of them. I am a great admirer of Fritz Lang, and he was foremost on my mind. Any film-maker who really cares about camera work owes a lot to Lang, and this goes for Welles as well as for Kubrick. He created images that are still present within us because they were so powerful, like that of a silhouette dominated by the architecture. So, I did in fact think about *Mabuse, M* and *Metropolis.* Another source of inspiration was *The Third Man* and, curiously enough, Howard Hawks for two or three scenes, like the one where Kafka leaves the café, comes across the anarchists and says: "Gabriela has disappeared." The conversation speeds up suddenly, everyone speaks at the same time, runs into each other, and I thought about *His Girl Friday.* I would have liked for the film to be more that way, with that kind of energy. I like that about Hawks, and also the fact he would jump from one genre to another. I hate to be cornered in only one type of film. I would like for people not to take *Kafka* too seriously, not to look for a deep analysis of a writer, and to see the humor in it, not only in the scenes with the twins, but also in those with Armin Mueller-Stahl. For me, when he says "Kafka," that calls up an entire world.

Q: *Like always, the humor comes from the gap between the world and our percep-tion of it.*

A : That's something else that attracted me to the script and connected it to *sex, lies, and videotape:* the feeling of disillusionment. No one turns out to be what you thought they were and this greatly frustrates Kafka. There is not a scene that unfolds the way he originally imagined it. He is surprised and disoriented every time. Jeremy Irons had never read Kafka when he was young, and according to him he is a writer one can appreciate when one is young. When he had to read him later in order to prepare for the film, he admitted to wanting to shake him up, to hit him so he would do something, so he would marry the girl. According to him, Kafka's obsessions are those of the eternal adolescent: someone who does not know how to talk to women, who is dominated by his father, etc. And I think that in a way he is right. Of course, there are other sides to him: the manipulation of the individual by the State and the more or less unconscious complicity with evil. For example, he accepts the inspector's version of Gabriela's death. Many people in the U.S. asked me about this, why he accepted the suicide theory when he knew it was not true. I think his reaction is ambiguous because it is not completely untrue. Someone who is an anarchist in this type of situation is committing a kind of suicide.

Q : *How did you work with Jeremy Irons?*
A : Before making the film he asked me what he should read by Kafka. I told him it was not necessary, that I did not want him to develop a character based on autobiographical details. We would call him Joe or Fred, see him more like a brother but not necessarily like Franz. It was like a dream that Lem Dobbs had of Kafka mixed with other visions. There is no doubt that the title creates a problem for American audiences. Many people think that it's going to be a very serious film and that they are going to fail an exam while watching it. In fact, for Dobbs and me, the film is an exploration of what the word—and by extension the man—Kafka means to us. I am really curious to know how things went in Europe. Curiously, from the very first reactions, people here seem more open than in the States to the liberties we took; they are less protective of Kafka's image.

Q : *In the credits you are listed as editor but under the rubric "picture editor" rather than "film editor." Was this for syndication reasons?*
A : No, it was simply in order to be more accurate because I did not edit the film on a flat bad but on video, like *sex, lies, and videotape.* During post-pro-

duction we speak of sound-editing and image-editing. Since I was in charge
of the latter, it seemed more pertinent to me. This is the part that I find the
most fun. I restructured the first ten minutes of the film. I also worked a lot
on the fourth reel. At first, we had the action spanning several days, but that
did not work. For instance, he was mugged in the elevator and the next
morning he would go back to work. It was strange. Now, this all takes place
in one evening and the next day he goes to the castle. What led me to make
this change is that in the first version everyone wanted me to cut the elevator
scene because they could not understand how he could go back to work as if
nothing had happened. Since it was one of my favorite scenes in the film, I
desperately wanted to keep it and come up with something else. In the film
you saw today, I established continuity between the moment when Jeremy
is sitting in the bathroom and the moment he is in his office and Joel Grey
(Burgel) tells him that he has to work late. He has a different shirt on, but
because it is in black and white I don't think anybody noticed.

Q: *Did you always have Jeremy Irons in mind for the role?*
A: He has always been one of my favorite actors. He was the only one I had
in mind for the role of Kafka, and I was lucky that he was free and that he
accepted to play the part without asking for a huge salary. It would have
depressed me to have to choose someone else. One of the great advantages
of the success of *sex, lies, and videotape* is that it made it possible for me to
meet people like Jeremy, Alec Guinness and Ian Holm, and that they knew
who I was. I talked to Jeremy Irons and, frankly, I don't think he really
thought there was material for a film here. He trusted me. It's not an easy
role to play because it's not spectacular in any way. His part is very passive;
he reacts more than he acts. The danger is to overdo it, particularly since we
don't shoot in chronological order. Jeremy was very conscious of this. He
loves crossword puzzles and he was really into them during the shooting.
One day, we were shooting in Alec Guinness's office, there were lots of people there, and we had to look for Jeremy for five minutes. Well, he was there,
in a corner of the room, doing crossword puzzles! He told me he got in the
habit of doing this because of the long hours of waiting on the set. At the
beginning when we started rolling, he tended to overdo it because he had
been thinking about the scene during his off hours. Thanks to the crossword
puzzle, he was able to approach the sequences by under-playing. He and I
share a preference for subtleties. He is a very smart, very meticulous person

who knows film very well. You can't dazzle him with technique and he likes to ask you questions about what you are going to do. This did not bother me at all, nor was I afraid to show my hesitations. He encouraged me not to be lazy and always made interesting suggestions. This was a very fruitful collaboration. I would not have wanted to be a director he did not respect because, as I said, he is very intelligent and has a strong presence due to his stature and his voice.

I would not want to be an actor and have to put up with a director doing to me what he spends his time doing with other actors. I can imagine how annoying it must be for a great actor to work for a director he does not respect. David Cronenberg told me about his experience as an actor in Clive Barker's *Cabal.* He couldn't stop asking himself why the director was doing this or that, why he had chosen this shot rather than another where he looked better. According to him, an actor only has his body and that makes you very self-conscious. At one point, he had to talk while crossing a room and he almost told Barker: "Do you want me to talk and to move at the same time!" Of course, everyone on the set would have laughed, but I can understand this pretty typical reaction from an actor. I would have reacted exactly like David, feeling totally powerless. In the States, people always ask me if I was intimidated working with Alec Guinness and Jeremy Irons, and I don't understand their question. They are professionals who agreed to play these parts, and I don't see why they would have wanted to attack me. But maybe American actors are different from European actors. Ian Holm told me he preferred being liked by the people he worked with than being thought of as a great actor. I like American actors a lot, but they tend to take on the character's personality and it becomes difficult for a director to manage them. European actors are better able to let go of their role at the end of the day and to go home. During the shooting of *Midnight Express,* Brad Davis asked John Hurt: "How do you manage to play your character?" And Hurt simply told him: "I pretend!" Americans think that if they do not become the character twenty-four hours a day, they'll lose a grip on him; which does not mean that British actors, for example, don't take their work seriously. In fact, Jeremy Irons is the perfect blend of the two approaches. He has the training and the experience that many British actors have because of their work in the theater, and at the same time, like many Method actors, he has no inhibitions and is ready to do anything, even if it means looking ridiculous, in

order to get somewhere. He knows how to be energetic and how to impro-
vise, if necessary.

Q: *The use of the cymbalum, the Hungarian instrument, in the musical score is
very original.*
A: I told Cliff Martinez that I wanted an instrument that was close to the
zither because it seemed to go well with the atmosphere of the place. I had a
Carol Reed experience. I was in a restaurant listening to a gypsy group playing the cymbalum and I knew this is what I was looking for. Cliff used a
numerical recording of a cymbalum, brought it back to the U.S. and he was
able to replay the sound of the cymbalum in his electric drum—he is a drum-
mer—while looking at the film on video. So many films nowadays overlook
the extent to which music can be used in counterpoint, and even in irony. I
think Cliff Martinez understands this very well.

Q: *Was the sculptor based on Max Brod?*
A: He was a synthesis of Kafka's friends. There is a reference to Brod in the
sense that he liked Kafka's work while the latter asked him to destroy it. I
think Max Brod was right. When Kafka would ask him to burn his writings,
it was a way for him to make this request at the same time knowing that he
wouldn't do it. Brod told him many times that he wouldn't do it, so I think
there was a tacit understanding between them.

Q: *It's strange that three recent Anglo-Saxon films*—Barton Fink, Naked Lunch,
and Kafka—*all deal with a similar theme: the corruption of the world by the imagination of a writer.*
A: What they have in common is that they evoke the world of the writer.
But the difference, I think, is that *Kafka* does not deal with literary creation.
It stops where the other two films begin. The implication, in *Kafka,* is that
these events will become a fiction, will inspire him, while *Naked Lunch* and
Barton Fink talk about the moment of inspiration, of creation. But it's true
that it's a strange coincidence, and just as strange that Woody Allen's *Shadow
and Frog* and *Kafka* are coming out at the same time. I don't think this is the
beginning of a trend and that producers are going to launch into imitations!
I don't know in what direction American Cinema is going, but I feel that

people in the business are worried and are not sure of anything. Movie tickets are so expensive that the public knows what to expect when they go see a studio film; but I don't think they are ready to take chances with a film like *Kafka*. By nature I am more pessimistic than optimistic, which is not a typically American attitude.

Interview with Steven Soderbergh: *King of the Hill*

MICHEL CIMENT AND HUBERT
NIOGRET/1993

Q: *You have surprised us once again with your third film* King of the Hill.
A: When I read the book in 1986, I was very attracted to the character of the boy, in some ways, I felt close to him. The fact that the story takes place in the thirties was of secondary interest to me, even though my father grew up during this period. He knows the popular culture well, has kept many records from the time and I owe to him my love for the cinema. This decade was very accessible to me and I felt very comfortable in relation to it. On the other hand, the social correspondences—economic crisis, unemployment— were not as evident as they are today when I first discovered Hotchner's text. So, there's a happy coincidence. Also, when I took on the project in 1989, I was not married yet and had no children. And, of course, that also influenced my approach to the subject. I knew the material was very different from my first two films, and this was part of its appeal.

Q: *When did the book come out?*
A: In 1972. Hotchner had been contacted many times by producers, but he had never wanted to sell the rights because it was very personal for him. Robert Redford, whose company was involved in the project in its initial stage, came to see Hotchner and succeeded in convincing him that he would not be disappointed. Once he accepted, he became very cooperative, very friendly, and he never reproached us for our choices to include or leave out this or that passage. In fact, the book is not very long, it does not have an

From *Positif,* October 1993. Translated by Paula Willoquet. Reprinted by permission.

epic structure, and I think you'll agree that as far as the tone and the emotions are concerned the film is very close to the book. Since the story uses the first person narration, everyone thought I was going to use a narrator. I knew, however, from the very beginning, that I would not. Unless you adopt a particular strategy for the narration—like in *Sunset Boulevard* or in Terrence Malick's two films, *Badlands* and *Days of Heaven* which make brilliant use of a narrator who is neither very conscious nor very eloquent—I don't really see the need for one. So, I had to achieve the same results by different means. On the one hand, I incorporated certain lines in the first person from the book into the dialogue so as to give a sense of the main character's personality. On the other hand, I simply invented things, like the imaginary story about Charles Lindbergh he tells in class at the beginning. This little speech enabled us to enter his world. Finally, I was lucky to find a young actor who was able to invoke interior thought. A narrator would tend to encourage you to read the events in a specific way, and I did not want any part of that. I wanted the audience to be freer in their interpretation.

Q: *You made a film based on an original script* (sex, lies, and videotape), *another based on someone else's script* (Kafka), *and now a third based on a novel. Do you encounter different kinds of problems with each?*

A: There are problems particular to each project, but I don't feel any closer to *sex, lies, and videotape* than to *King of the Hill,* for example. It's true that at first I was a bit terrified at the thought of tackling someone else's work in order to adapt it for the screen. I adopted a method that William Goldman suggested, which is to read the text with a color pen and to underline what must absolutely be kept; then to read it again twice more with different color pens. Then, the passages that have been underlined in three colors should make it into the film. I ended up with a short version of the book in the form of a script that was unfilmable! This set me free to invent, to establish connections that did not exist in Hotchner's text. But this first stage, in spite of not being very productive, was useful to me because I was afraid to distance myself from the book, to imagine. When Hotchner read the script, he had to admit that it was at the same time different from and similar to what he had written. Emotionally, it was faithful to the original. So, it was a difficult process, but not as difficult as starting from scratch with a blank page, as with *sex, lies, and videotape.* As for *Kafka,* the problem was to film a script by someone who is very smart and very stubborn, like a family member with whom you have no control. We plan to work together again, but I told Lem Dobbs that in the meantime he should make a film so he might gain more, or less, appreciation for what I do, because right now he is in the enviable position of never having made a film and of knowing it all. These three films then posed different problems. I suppose, also, with *sex, lies, and videotape* my collaborators were less inclined to send me notes, to offer comments; they felt I was very close to the material. So, they hesitated telling me what to do. With the other two films, I got many more suggestions.

Q : *Since Hotchner's book is an autobiographical fragment, did you ask him to tell you something about the characters' background, about what does not appear in the book?*

A : In this sense too, he was very cooperative. I showed him the script two weeks before we started shooting, and he gave me information about incidents that are not in the text. Also, when he visited the set, he would talk to the actors about their characters and his anecdotes, his digressions, the background details were very useful. For example, at the beginning, when they visit the new apartment, the younger brother calls out to his older brother: "Can you hear me?" Hotchner told us it was great for them because, up until then, they had lived in a one-room apartment; so, to call out to each other from one room to another was unheard of. His comments also addressed the film that I was making rather than the film that I should have made, according to him. I appreciated his support at a time when, in America, it's fashionable for authors to pretend that we have ruined their work. The brother does not appear in the book; he had already left before the beginning. I felt it was necessary for him to appear in the film because the separation of the brothers carries a great emotional weight for Aaron. His physical presence at the opening of the film seemed crucial since his younger brother constantly referred to him, and also at the end when he returns. I also collapsed two characters into one in the case of Mr. Mungo, played by Spalding Gray, who lives across the hall. I had to invent dialogue for him. I really like the sequences that take place in this room, and I would have liked to shoot an entire film with this Fassbinder-like atmosphere, where a child is confronted with a strange situation which he does not really understand, with these two characters who seem to hate each other but who have a physical relationship based on money.

Q : *What most fundamentally made you want to shoot this film?*

A : I shared the child's feelings. My parents are divorced and did not get along, even if everything took place behind closed doors. In this child's emotional confusion about the behavior of the adults, I found what I had felt as a child. Even I could not understand the reason for their actions. I saw two beings that clearly did not get along but continued to live together, stay together. I would ask myself: If they are together, they must love each other, but it doesn't look like they love each other. This idea, coupled with the idea that this child seemed to be the only adult in the story, appealed to me. I also like the aesthetic dimension of the period, the decor, the music. What most attracted me was the fact that this kid lived in his thoughts, which was the case for me too.

Q : *In your reconstruction of the period, you chose not to show the sordid side of reality caused by the economic conditions during the Depression.*
A : First of all, Hotchner's book, no matter how much imagination you apply to it, is not *Grapes of Wrath*. Then, there was a lot of optimism at that time. People had not become cynical, they had not been betrayed by their government yet, nor caught up in a shady conflict that had ended badly. As Hotchner used to say to me, he never thought he would not be able to make it. The community had a faith in the future, in spite of all the adversity, which no longer exists today. You cannot forget that the action is set at a time when Roosevelt comes to power, many jobs are created, and there is hope for a new beginning. Which does not mean that my point of view is devoid of pessimism. For me, the story was leading up to this sequence where he found himself abandoned by everyone and alone in this room, eating pages from the newspaper advertising food, which ends up giving him hallucinations. This had to be a trying scene. What is strange about his predicament is that he never weighs the danger he is in, because kids don't have a sense of their own mortality. And I wanted to shoot the story from his perspective, the perspective of a 12-year-old boy who does not know what the Depression means, and who thinks that's just the way things are, particularly since his family was never well-off, even with the Depression. I don't know if I succeeded in getting the idea across that what saves him at the end, strangely enough, is this kind of hallucination he has, stretched out on the floor in a semi-catatonic state, practically ready to die when he sees the candles. The anger he feels rising up in him against his father is what gets him out of his

stupor. Once he is able to express this anger, his situation improves, his father and brother return.

Q: *Like the James Spader character in* sex, lies, and videotape, *and like* Kafka, *he is not in sync with the world.*
A: Absolutely. If there is a link among the three films, it lies with the main characters that are out of sync with their environment. I am attracted to these mental states. I was struck by the little game that the critics and film folks at the [Cannes Film] Festival played to find out whether I was really an "auteur." This makes me laugh because I think you can only know this once a filmmaker has made twenty films. A Huston or a Hawks were never fashionable, and they expressed themselves through a variety of genres. I'm not a visionary artist; sometimes I would like to be, but I don't belong to that category of filmmakers like Kubrick, Altman, or Fellini, let alone share their talent. These artists have changed the cinematic vocabulary; their films are unlike any others. I am more like those who respond to a certain kind of subject matter, and who look for the best style to express it. I am not trying to impose my style. It's like the difference between studio films and independent films, as if the independents were always great while the studio owners were always the bad guys. I think that some critics, instead of trying to appear confident, should admit that they can be bewildered by a filmmaker's choice. Of course, it's always easier to avoid this by simply stating that you weren't expecting this or that from the filmmaker and that you are not interested. Human beings are complicated machines. There are days I feel closer to Kafka, others I feel closer to the kid: I change from one day to the next.

Q: *How did you envision the hotel, which is different from the one in* Barton Fink?
A: It's certainly present in the book. In *Barton Fink,* the Coen brothers really turned the hotel into a character. Their hotel was almost the hero. My hotel had to assert itself by degrees, culminating in a scene which was secondary to the plot, and which I completely cut out. Aaron was locked up in his room toward the end of the film, then he came down to the dancing room in the basement and asked for a job at the "customer service" desk, an expression he had heard from a prostitute. It was an extremely baroque scene, with everybody sweating, dominated by blue, a color that is never present in the film. Visually, it was very striking, but I had to cut it out: first, because the

film was too long; then, you could ask why he was able to leave his room to ask this but not to steal food, since he was dying of hunger. I couldn't put the scene elsewhere either because it was linked to his physical and mental state.

Q : *How long was the first cut?*
A : Two hours and fifteen minutes. It was very long and I cut thirty-five minutes. I don't like films that are long only because the director was too attached to what he filmed. The length of *Lawrence of Arabia* is justified, but *King of the Hill* is not an epic. I like to leave the theater wanting to see the film again. I had a lot of difficulties making cuts, including cutting this sequence, but I think it was in the interest of the film. It's interesting to see how often the audience is ahead of you and able to make connections, and often they don't understand at all what you are trying to do because your intentions are too intimately connected to who you are as a director. I don't ask that the audience like what I do, but I insist that they understand it.

Q : *You chose warm colors—browns, yellows, amber tones.*
A : We followed Edward Hopper, where the reds are burgundy, the yellows are mustard. The neighborhood in St. Louis where we shot had those tonalities; the bricks were a strong uniform red. I never saw so much brick in my life. We deliberately limited the range of colors, and we took great care with the texture of the walls and ceilings, with their smooth surfaces reflecting light. It was very different from the "realist" tones of *sex, lies, and videotape* or from the black and white of *Kafka,* let alone from the strange and cold colors in the latter's final sequence. It's interesting to see how you can influence the audience indirectly through sound and color. It makes me sick to see films where the set and sound designers have not really made a contribution, which of course, in the final analysis, is the director's fault. Of course, sets cost a lot and the artistic director has more financial constraints than the cinematographer. You don't need a lot of lights to light your set well, as shown by Philippe Rousselot. The director has to be very clear and specific about what he wants from his set designer if he wants his work to come across in the image. That's why I tend to be well prepared, and to plan and construct the scenes in advance. I don't shoot thousands of feet of film only to work it all out in the editing. I have to be able to say that I don't need a ceiling for these scenes, or that I'll need half a ceiling in another scene. Little

details like this make it possible for you to come to the set the day before and to ask that a surface be repainted. Changes like this can only happen if you've already taken account of them in your budget. For *King of the Hill*, we had a budget of eight million dollars for eight weeks of shooting. The hotel was built in a warehouse. Overall, we tried to be faithful to the style of the period, avoiding colors that were too familiar to contemporary audiences. We were not looking for a photographic style like that of Walker Evans. The fact that we were dealing with recollections gave us more freedom. Times were hard, but by the same token the memories were tainted with nostalgia. My father, for example, is still drawn to this period.

Q : *Did you have films of this period in mind?*
A : Not really. We were looking for an emotional quality that was linked to childhood. We referenced *The Four Hundred Blows, The Bicycle Thief, My Life as a Dog*, or even *Hope and Glory* that also evokes a dramatic period in a strange way.

Q : *How do you explain the tendency nowadays to make films about childhood memories, from* Radio Days *to* Reunion, Empire of the Sun *and Kubrick's forthcoming* Wartime Lies *[ed. note: the film was never made.]?*
A : It may have something to do with the breakdown of the family, the increasing number of divorces, children born of different marriages. The result is my generation, fractured, without direction. I was led to study the huge psychological impact that an unstable, unpredictable, uncertain education can have. I don't know if other filmmakers had the same reaction, but this certainly played a role for me. I think my father's generation valued sacrifices more highly. Nowadays, many adults in America, at a certain point in their lives, decide to think about themselves first, to have a new wife, etc. I am not passing judgment, but I am sure this has affected these people's children. For a long time the effects were hidden, but they are coming to the surface now. We have a generation of kids who don't care about other human beings, who don't feel any connection with others because in their own lives these connections were severed very early on.

Q : *How did you work with Jesse Bradford who plays Aaron?*
A : He was amazing, independently of his professional experience. There is a saying in Hollywood that you should never work with water, planes, ani-

mals, and kids. After *sex, lies, and videotape,* there was no greater challenge
for me than to make *Kafka.* After *Kafka,* it was another challenge to get a
great performance from a child actor. He is in every scene and carries the
entire film. With our tiny budget we looked in three cities, in the manner of
Gone with the Wind. The first kid I auditioned was Jesse Bradford. I told the
casting director: "That's him." Twenty minutes after I had chosen who
would play the part of Lester, she told me: "Stop! I am not going to let you
decide after only one audition!" Particularly since we still had three weeks to
decide! I told her it was not my fault that she had done a great job. But she
was panicking anyway. And it went on like that: Jeroen Krabbe, Lisa Eichhorn, Spalding Gray, Elizabeth McGovern, Karen Allen were all my first
choices. They were free so I was able to hire them. What struck me about
Jesse Bradford is that there was like a veil over his face when he was reading
the script or talking to me. He was curious and professional, but he was not
letting me see how he felt about what was happening to his character in the
film, nor how he was affected by the experience of making this film. It was
as if he was wearing a mask for the audition, and that's exactly what his
character would have done. My only problem was his good looks that might
have made it more difficult for people to identify with his plight, unless he
could compensate for that with some unusually good acting. Which he succeeded in doing.

Q : *The title,* King of the Hill, *is very mysterious.*
A : I like the irony in it. There is a point in the book tied to this expression.
When he is eating paper and has hallucinations, he is dreaming that he is
playing this well-known game in the States: a kid who is standing on a hill
has to fight off his playmates who are trying to make him fall so they can
take his place as "king of the hill." In this dream, which becomes a nightmare, he is on a hill made of mud and a mudslide buries the two kids who
were trying to dislodge him. This was part of the first version of the film; I
had to leave it out. But I kept the title as a counterpoint because he is everything but king of the hill. I thought it had a nice ring to it.

Q : *It's not part of the American tradition for the director to be the editor as well.
However, you seem to always work that way.*
A : I think that if film directors wanted to do it, they could. In fact, most of
them are in the editing room. It's true that from a practical standpoint the

syndicates don't like that, and it is out of the question that I get paid for my work as editor. The prices are set by the editors' Guild and they don't like it that I edit my own films. But, for me, it's during the editing process that film becomes an art. You bring all the elements together and you build the film. It's the part I like best. Sometimes I like directing, but I love editing. When I edit, I sometimes resent directors, but I like it anyway.

Q : *From this perspective, what was it like to make* King of the Hill?
A : King of the Hill was hard work. I started the adaptation while I was finishing *Kafka*. Then I staged it and shot more film than I had ever before, with a script that was unusually long. The film had a more open structure than the first two, and I constantly had to solve many different problems. The shooting was exhausting because I really had nobody to back me up, although I can't say there were no pressures on me. Then, I had to sit down everyday for months at the editing table. I have two projects, one rather modest and the other more ambitious. This time, I think I'll hire an editor to work while we are shooting; this will keep me from having to reshoot certain scenes, which is very expensive. I have just finished shooting a film "noir" about a half hour long, *The Quiet Room,* based on a novel which I knew nothing about, written under the pseudonym of Jonathan Craig, a name which I was not familiar with either! I had liked the story and I proposed it to a cable station, Showtime, that was producing a series of six short films, *Fallen Angels,* based on novelists like Chandler, Hammett or Cain, and directed by Jonathan Kaplan, Phil Joanou, Alfonso Cuaron, Tom Hanks and Tom Cruise. They had hired an editor and that disoriented me. In fact, if I shoot a dialogue sequence with three consecutive scenes, I know exactly at what point I am going to connect them. I was intrigued to find out whether they would know that too, and most of the time they did not. He was not a bad editor, but I understood then the extent to which I was already editing with the camera.

Q : *Can you tell us more about these two projects?*
A : The most important one from the point of view of budget deals with the beginnings of professional football in the twenties. The second is an original idea that I'm going to try to develop this summer. It's going to be very strange and contemporary, that's all I can tell you now. I have been thinking about if for a long time. I haven't stopped taking notes without really know-

ing whether it's going to amount to anything. I didn't want the film to express the theme I had in mind overtly. It's an even more personal project than *sex, lies, and videotape,* what disappoints me is that the ideas behind the film are the same ideas *in* the film. Fundamentally, the characters are the ones who articulate the ideas. I would like to achieve something more oblique. One day, while I was walking the streets of New York, all of a sudden I understood how to accomplish this. At the same time, I was frustrated because I was almost done editing *King of the Hill* and I had to shoot that episode for television and after that I had to come to Cannes and did not have a chance to tackle that script. I only want one thing right now, and it's to get to work. Up until now, I have not made a great film, something that really corresponds to my own notions of the cinematographic art. I hope this project will allow me to explore a territory that is personal, something you can only do after years of practice and experience.

Steven Soderbergh Hopes That Three Is His Lucky Number

KENNETH M. CHANKO/1993

WRITER-DIRECTOR STEVE SODERBERGH, whose new movie, *King of the Hill* opens Friday, says he's been thinking a lot these days about John Singleton, whose second film, *Poetic Justice* opened this summer.

"It's funny. Here I am, all of 30 years old," says Soderbergh with a laugh, "and I find myself feeling very paternalistic toward guys like John and Quentin [Tarantino, writer-director of *Reservoir Dogs*]. I feel like calling them up and telling them, 'Hey, because you got so much attention from your first movie, you'll be walking into a buzzsaw with your second movie, no matter what you do, so just get on with it and make another film as soon as you possibly can.' "

Soderbergh's is one of the more recent voices of experience when it comes to the subject of directors and sophomore jinxes. Following his critically acclaimed debut film, the 1989 *sex, lies, and videotape*, Soderbergh made *Kafka* two years ago. The highly stylized black-and-white film, which starred Jeremy Irons, was not well received by the critics and went nowhere at the box office. Acting on his own advice, Soderbergh proceeded directly to *King of the Hill*, a film that may reestablish Soderbergh's reputation as one of this country's more talented young filmmakers.

Based on A. E. Hotchner's 1972 memoir, *King of the Hill* is something of a cross between *Barton Fink* and *This Boy's Life*. Set in St. Louis in 1933 and taking place predominantly in a seedy hotel, the film focuses on Aaron (Jesse

Bradfield), an imaginative 12-year-old whose mother (Lisa Eichhorn) is in poor health and whose distracted father (Jeroen Krabbe) is having difficulties finding a substantial job. So Aaron, whose younger brother (Cameron Boyd) is shipped off to relatives early in the film, is left to his own devices as he encounters eccentric neighbors like Mr. Mungo (Spalding Gray), a fellow trying to keep up appearances as he entertains a paid-for companion (Elizabeth McGovern) in his room.

Seven years ago, Soderbergh read the book by Hotchner and was immediately interested in adapting it—only to discover that Hotchner had no interest in selling the rights. One of the rewards for the success of *sex, lies,* though, was getting to meet Robert Redford's people, who were interested in what Soderbergh wanted to do next. By one of those coincidences that make networking go, Redford was a friend of Hotchner's and wound up helping persuade the writer that Soderbergh was the right man to bring the story of his youth to the screen.

"It must have been difficult for him, because it's such a personal story," says Soderbergh of the author (who's best known for another memoir, *Papa Hemingway,* about Hotchner's famous writer friend and compatriot). "It's become fashionable for authors to distance themselves from the films that have been made from their books, but from the beginning, Hotchner was gracious and really supportive. After I showed him the script, instead of questioning why this was changed or why that wasn't included, he made suggestions based on what was there—little things that we could use."

As for the period, Soderbergh felt more than comfortable about doing a film set during the Depression. "My father grew up in that period," he says. "He's a historian of 78 rpm records and has written books on the subject. And he's a real film nut. So I didn't feel like a dilettante walking around in that time. It was all very fresh to me because my father was steeped in it. Whereas, on *Kafka,* I felt more like a dilettante."

Soderbergh was born in Georgia and lives in Virginia with his wife, actress Betsy Brantley (*Five Days One Summer, Havana*), and their 2-year-old daughter. He lived in Pennsylvania, Boston, Texas and Virginia before his father, an academic, settled down at Louisiana State University. It was in Baton Rouge, at age 13, that Soderbergh borrowed camera equipment from film students at LSU and began making short films. "Seeing *Jaws* when I was 12 made me think about making movies," says Soderbergh. "I was so affected by that movie, and I remember thinking when I walked out of the theater, 'Who did this to me? Who were the people who made this movie?' I was always an obsessive kid. Before movies, it was baseball. I would sleep in my baseball uniform."

Soderbergh, who never went to college ("Making short films on my own while I was in high school was my movie education," he says), moved to Hollywood in the summer of 1980 and got various editing jobs, mostly recutting programs for Showtime. But that work soon dried up, and he recalls tough times toward the end of his first—and so far only—year in Hollywood. "Let's say I wasn't exactly living the good life in Hollywood," he says. "At one point, I remember being between jobs and having no money. I went over to a buddy's house because he had a jar of jelly, which was more than I had."

Before moving back to Baton Rouge to develop his screenwriting hand and shoot more short films, Soderbergh directed a feature-length concert movie for the rock band Yes, which was enough to get him an agent. By the time he had written a couple of scripts, one being *sex, lies,* Soderbergh was able to get the film into production for the summer of 1988.

Though his first three features seem starkly different, Soderbergh believes there is a discernible link.

"The films share protagonists who feel isolated from their surroundings and who find themselves at odds with people around them," he says.

Soderbergh admits to having similar feelings as a teen-ager. His parents were divorced when he was 16; but to him, he says, the question was always "Why did they wait that long? I was completely confused by their behavior. I know they weren't happy, but I didn't know why. They were together, and had six kids [Soderbergh being the second youngest], but they didn't seem to want to be together. I shared that with Aaron in *King of the Hill,* that feeling of never quite being able to get my bearings when it came to my parents.

"Part of the movie," Soderbergh adds, "is about realizing that your parents aren't the idealized people you once thought they were. For most of us, that probably doesn't happen until our late teens, when we started having our own relationships, but Aaron, because of his circumstances, goes through this compressed period of disillusionment."

Soderbergh, who shot *King of the Hill* during the summer of 1992 in and around St. Louis, is currently working on several projects. He's preparing a comedy tentatively titled *Leatherheads,* which he describes as "a Preston

Sturges/Howard Hawks-type comedy about the early days of professional football." He's also writing a screenplay, a variation on the 1949 film noir *Criss Cross,* that he plans to executive-produce but not direct. Then comes directing *A Confederacy of Dunces,* the New Orleans-set comedy based on John Kennedy Toole's acclaimed 1980 novel, whose protagonist can be fairly described as being at odds with those around him.

Soderbergh wants, of course, nothing but the best for *King of the Hill,* yet based on previous experience, he's aware that his perceptions of his career don't always match critics' expectations. "I don't consider myself an artist or a visionary," he says matter-of-factly. "There are the Fellinis, the Altmans— even someone like Gus Van Sant—who push the film language, who bend and twist the medium to suit their vision. You look at their movies and you can't imagine anyone else making them. I'm not that kind of filmmaker. I'm a chameleon. Style is secondary to me. I go with the material and then sit down and think about what style would best suit that material.

"I think that was part of the reason for the critical backlash against *Kafka,* which I knew had a bull's-eye on it in terms of its subject matter and style. People who imagined a certain career for me based on *sex, lies* were hoping they'd have this guy around, maybe Woody Allen kind of thing, every 18 months. They wanted that, but that's not who I am. *Sex, lies* required a style of assuming a Woody Allen-type persona, but for *Kafka* the style had to be different, and now for *King of the Hill* the style is, again, different."

Although he's not counting on it, Soderbergh can't help musing that, just maybe, "After I do this sports comedy, which will require another different style, people will start to get it."

Interview with Steven Soderbergh: *The Underneath*

MICHEL CIMENT AND HUBERT NIOGRET/1995

Q : *When you wrote the script for* The Underneath, *which you signed with the pseudonym of Sam Lowry, you had no intentions of making the film yourself?*
A : When I was finishing editing *King of the Hill,* Universal called me to say that they were thinking about remaking *Criss Cross,* which I had never seen. When I watched it, I thought it would be an interesting script to write, that I could bring some ideas to it, but I told them that I didn't really want to direct it. I wrote the scripts for two of my first three films and that's something I like to do. On top of that, I needed work. I also liked the idea of writing for someone else and of seeing what they would do with it. Half way through the writing, I realized that there were certain elements in the script that were particular to me, and I wasn't at all sure that a third party would know what I had in mind. So I called Universal to tell them that I was planning to direct it myself. It happened like that, by chance. It's not one of those kinds of projects you think about for years. Everything happened very fast after that. I finished the script and we began shooting.

Q : *Why did you write under a pseudonym?*
A : I had a conflict with the Writers' Guild, following a ruling they passed on the script. The Guild's rule is that you send them the credits for the script once the film is done. If they notice that the director or the producer is trying to get credit for the script, there has to be a ruling automatically. The fact that I was the only scriptwriter did not seem to matter to them. Their deci-

From *Positif,* April 1996. Translation by Patricia Willoquet. Reprinted by permission.

sion was that my name and that of Daniel Fuchs should appear in the opening credits. I told them that I thought that was pretty stupid since Fuchs had
been dead for thirty-five years and that would give the impression that we
had collaborated on the script! My suggestion was that we indicate that I had
written the script based on Don Tracy's novel and on Daniel Fuchs's script
for the first version of the film. The Guild refused. According to the rules, I
had twenty-four hours to ask for a hearing, but I had been traveling and
came back after the deadline. I couldn't object anymore so in order to voice
my disagreement and my dissatisfaction, I signed using a pseudonym using
the name of one of the characters in *Brazil*. That seemed an appropriate
response to the bureaucracy!

Q: *What was your response to* Criss Cross?
A: I watched the film without really studying it. There were two things that
I wanted to use: the idea of a man coming back home and wanting to reestab-
lish a rapport with his ex-wife, and the hospital scene. I changed the family
interactions quite a bit, and I invented a past for the two protagonists. In
Criss Cross, you don't see what the relationship between Burt Lancaster and
Yvonne de Carlo has been like, and as a spectator I would have wanted to
know.

Q: *Was it a challenge for you to tackle for the first time a film with a defined
genre and constraints, and a remake on top of that?*
A: I like this kind of film. I also like the fact that *sex, lies, and videotape* was
an original script, *Kafka* was based on someone else's script, *King of the Hill*
was inspired by a novel, and *The Underneath* is a remake. It makes sense to
me to try anything once. When I started working on *The Underneath,* I
thought the film would be much more of a thriller than it turned out to be.
I did not know at first that there would be so much of me in the film. I
thought I was going to be able to adapt the film in a traditional way, which
is what they hired me to do. That's really what I wanted to do, but I suppose
it was stronger than I thought and I realize now that from the very beginning
I have been making the same film four times, even if it does not seem that
way to others. I also could say that, ironically, Michael's character in *The
Underneath* is more like me than any other character in my other films. He is
incapable of living in the present. And I like to think that's also the case for
the first two thirds of the film; the film and the character have the same

problem. In the United States, where the film did not work well, many people were confused by the last third, which is different from the rest.

Q : *What appealed to you about the film noir style?*
A : There is a central idea in this genre that I like a lot: a character lives as a function of a certain number of values in which he/she believes, and in relation to a moral code. When they start to want something very strongly, just for a moment they think they can cross that line that they themselves established in order to get what they want, and then go back to the way things were. Naturally, they find out that's not possible. It's a recurring theme in all the films of this genre that I like. On the other hand, the exterior aspects or the genre don't really interest me. From the very beginning I told my collaborators: no wet pavement, no huge shadows, no hats, no smoke. That's not what I was looking for. So we spent our time talking about colors and space. Many filmmakers today are trying to imitate the visual aspects of the noir genre, but that seems pointless to me. Of course, when I watched them, I had an appreciation for the shadows and all the rest, but at the emotional level what stayed with me was the moral dilemma at the heart of the story. You have to acknowledge the conventions associated with this kind of film if you decide to make one, but most importantly, you have to bring your own point of view. The only one in the States to have seen a major difference between *The Underneath* and the classics from half a century ago may have been Todd McCarthy in his review for *Variety.* He made the remark that in those films it's always destiny or chance that is responsible for the tragic end, whereas in *The Underneath* it's the character who, because of a series of decisions, brings about his own downfall. Michael is someone who spent his entire life refusing to take responsibility for his actions. In the end, he dug his own grave. This is a fundamental difference between this film and the original where Burt Lancaster can't stop blaming bad luck. I kept this idea to the extent that I made a gambler out of the character, so his life is dependent on luck, but at the same time I show that he has the choice to be a gambler or not. And that he ends up a prisoner of his choice.

Q : *Your title,* The Underneath, *is unlike the traditional film noir titles that call attention to visual aspects:* The Dark Corner, Asphalt Jungle, Panic in the Streets.

A: I chose it, in fact, in order to give a clue as to the interpretation. We were trying to go under the surface. I don't know if it was a good thing to encourage people to think along those lines. In any case, I did not want to deceive the audience by making them think this would be an action film, with chases around the big city. I really wanted to tone down the emotions. I decided to shoot in Austin, Texas, a city that does not really have a face. It's just a place where you live. This seemed to me to reflect Michael's point of view, his lack of interest in his physical environment; he doesn't think about it, he doesn't even pay attention to it. That's why the house, the streets, even the clothes are not very interesting. He is so concerned with his own problems that he doesn't notice anything around him. That did not keep me from wanting to give each place a particular physical presence, but once again, in a very controlled way. What interested me most above all this was the relationship among the characters, and particularly within this family that I find very strange.

Q: *While you were writing the script were you thinking about the colors already?*
A: Not at first. Half way through the writing, when I started organizing the structure and therefore the temporal levels, I started to imagine different chromatic possibilities to represent different periods of time. It was also at that point that I decided I did not want someone else shooting the film. I suppose that, like many writers, I did not want anyone disrupting what I had elaborated. Originally, there were four temporal levels; the first edit took account of all four but that was too confusing. It was a kind of flash-forward. At the beginning of the film, in the alley, the evening of the hold-up when they are discussing their plans and the color red is evoked, there are fragments of this fourth temporal level. Michael was saying things he would repeat at the end. But even my film crew didn't understand anything.

Q: *Why did you choose to shoot the burglary, which is in the present, using colors one generally associates with flashbacks?*
A: We talked about it. It's true that the past is generally more stylized, whereas we were doing the opposite. We used Ektachrome, which is a reversible stock and not very sensitive, and we overexposed and developed it as if it were a negative. Until my director of photography had told me, I did not know that reversible stock goes through two stages. In the first stage, the stock is developed like a negative, and in the second it's transformed into a

positive. We simply eliminated the second stage. Then, while we were editing, we learned from Kodack—nobody before us had used Ektachrome as a negative—that they had done some experiments on this stock with accelerated aging and that it was going to favor the greens. We asked: "When?" and they said: "Now!" We had to speed things up, pull the film, and from this interpositive we had to make a positive. I could see that between the time we shot and made a working copy—which was done right away—and the time we made the first release copy, which I saw four months later, the difference was astounding. It had been radically altered. What happens is that in the second stage of development into a positive, the development is interrupted. If you cut out this second stage, the film continues to develop and you can't stop it. Spike Lee heard about what we were doing and he called me. I showed him a few scenes and he ended up shooting a large portion of *Clockers* with Ektachrome.

To go back to your question, I wanted to stylize the present because I wanted to create a tension. This stock produced strange colors and a graininess that evoked a sense of anxiety and ill at ease. With Elliot Davis, my cinematographer, we wondered what color on the screen would produce the greatest discomfort, and we ended up deciding it was green. So we ran some tests with the Ektachrome and we decided to use it after we saw what was happening to the colors. And, to that, we added the hand held camera for the scenes in the present, and we ended up with the tension I wanted. You had to create that tension visually because, at the beginning, there is no logical reason why the spectator should feel uncomfortable. We had to suggest a premonition and that's what happened with the opening scene in the truck: the colors, the exchange of looks, the car which he can't stop noticing, etc.

Q: *Given the difficulty in controlling the film stock, how did you work out the relationship with the decor, where the strangeness of certain colors, particularly on one of the walls of the family's house, is connected to the overall chromatic ambiance?*
A: We ran a lot of tests and we obtained samples of all the colors we were planning on using, whether paint or filters, in order to see what would happen when we used Ektachrome. For the distant past, we eliminated the filters we usually use to shoot daylight in order to get a cold image. For the overall coloring, we made extensive preparations in order to see how each color

would come across in each of the three visual registers corresponding to the three temporal zones. I wanted each location to have a particular texture. I hate those films in which the place where the protagonist lives looks like the place where he works (or his friends' house), where everything is lit and painted in the same way. This doesn't correspond to my experience of the real world, where light is constantly changing. I like the visual density of *The Underneath*, as far as the colors and the lighting. It's a sign of laziness not to take advantage of elements like the light, or color, which do not cost anything.

Q: *How did you approach the scene with the armored vehicle? It's a classic situation in gangster films.*

A: I watched *The Killing*, which I like a lot, and particularly the structure, even though I wasn't taken with the voice over. I also screened *Asphalt Jungle*, which I also like, and I was obsessed with the Sterling Hayden slang: "You're trying to bone me?" an expression he repeats throughout the film. My decision to adopt this temporal structure had more to do with emotions than with narrative structure. Our existence is reflected in the film in the sense that our physical bodies go through life in a chronological, linear way from birth to death, while in the mind it's different. Every time something happens to us, we think about a similar experience in the past and we imagine the consequences in the future. There is a constant back and forth. Our minds are totally non-linear. It seemed interesting to try to express that in film. I had been dreaming of making a film where there would be no end to the dialogue, where the last sentence in a scene would lead to the first sentence of the next scene. It would have been like one uninterrupted conversation that would cut across the three temporal levels, a verbal flow analogous to the interior monologue. I tried but I did not succeed. I also realized that if I succeeded in doing this I was foreclosing any possibilities for change in the editing room. I acknowledge that film is a more emotional than intellectual medium of expression, but in this case, I get as much satisfaction from seeing a mosaic being built as from being scared by a shark in another film. As I spectator, I derive as much pleasure. But, in the United States in particular, the public tends to feel that if you implicate them in an intellectual process the film becomes cold. It's quite probable that, aside from *sex, lies, and videotape* where there is enough going on superficially to keep the spectator from entering into a process of reflection, the mental narrative in *Kafka, King of the Hill,* and *The Underneath* poses problems for the spectator.

The times do not favor a filmmaker like me; the proof of this is in the films that are popular. I don't know where the spectators for my films are: maybe they are home reading or watching films on video. Before we made *The Underneath,* the head of Universal told me he thought maybe there wasn't an audience for this kind of film here in the States. He was probably right. Luckily, it only cost 6.5 million dollars. The studio likes me and they want me to go on working with them, hoping one day I'll make a film people will want to see! I think they see me as a lost leader. This expression comes from the record industry. If there is a really good record that nobody wants to buy, the record store reduces the price, even if it means losing money, hoping that the promotional sale will bring people into the store that will then buy other records. I think I am a lost leader for Universal, and other filmmakers might say: "if they make a film with Soderbergh, maybe it's a good place to go work." With *King of the Hill* it will have been the second time I do this for them.

I think I came to the end of a cycle and now I am going to embark on a completely different territory. I would like to make small budget films that are experimental, that may not draw a large audience, or no audience at all. In fact, I just finished a film with a crew of five people, which might look like something conceived by Buñuel and Richard Lester! Something exuberant but not necessarily logical. I already sold the video rights in the U.S., which gave me enough money to shoot it, about 75,000 dollars. I am editing it now. In a way, I have left the movie business and I've freed myself from many things. I went back to Louisiana and I put together a small group of people to start from scratch. While making *The Underneath* I felt the need to start all over: I became aware of the kind of film I would like to make next and for which I was not until now prepared, for reasons that maybe have to do with my life or my profession. In fifteen years, people will look back at my first four films and they will realize that they were just a preface to a book that I am only now starting to write. Some of my personality traits, like my ideas, have not yet found a path to the screen, and some people who know me well ask me why. In a way, what I want to do will look a lot like the short films I made when I was young.

Q : *Your use of music is rather economical.*

A : I think that in American cinema, of all the elements, sound is the most badly used. It's as if it had to be put to work for the spectator. I wanted the music to contribute to the atmosphere in *The Underneath.* I was very happy when Cliff Martinez sent me what he had written for the credits. There was a sense of slowness to it analogous to Bernard Herrmann that fit the film well. Then, we set together and I pointed out to him the spots where I wanted the music to gently underscore the mood. I don't think the music needs to manipulate the audience. Cliff Martinez was remarkable and he worked very fast. I told him about a contemporary piece I had used and asked him to come up with something similar, without risking a lawsuit. I wanted an arrangement of notes with more weight than normal fourteen to sixteen. We worked at Cliff's with his electronic equipment, composing pieces, twenty maybe, with guitar sounds and we numbered them. Then we looked at a scene and tried out a sequence against it, let's say 2-7-9. Then we focused on the basic line, either trying to harmonize or create an opposition. We went through the entire film this way, scene by scene, note by note, and sometimes we took up the main motif in the credits and reworked it in a different arrangement. We had very little time because, initially, I didn't want any music at all, until I realized a little too late that it would have been a mistake. That's the reason why we were racing against the clock and we nailed down the music in eight days.

Q : *Everything seems to have happened fast with this film.*

A : There are positive things about this speed, the energy you save all along, the tension, but there are also negative sides, the lack of time to think things through, to step back. There is a better balance with the new film that I am finishing up. I have a script, but if it does not work out I can afford to put it in the trash and shoot something else. The only expense is the film stock, since I am working with five people and the equipment was bought very cheaply. When the crew has some free time I shoot, and that's how it goes. You have a lot of freedom this way, particularly since I don't have a firm deadline by which the film has to be finished, since I am not working with a studio. I don't have to release it if I don't like it! I can always write a script for someone else, which would enable me to pay back the cost for the video rights. Under these conditions there are only two limitations: my imagination and finding a topic that you can shoot with a small crew. I was a little tired of working with those huge crews of fifty people, who are like an albatross tied around your neck that you have to drag behind you and that limits your freedom of action. I was also tired of having to use the cinematic language that is required of a "normal" film, the establishing shot, the close up, etc. I really needed a new start.

Q: *How did you select your actors?*
A: I wrote the script with Peter Gallagher in mind. I called him and told him he would be perfect for the role of a great kid who was not worth much. He told me that sounded great. I am very happy with his performance: it's very realistic, without mannerism. It's a part that does not call for a lot of external action, and he played it out with a lot of subtlety and control. I stayed close to him during the shooting. He was more relaxed than when we did *sex, lies, and videotape*. I think he understands he'll never be a superstar, he'll not reach great notoriety, but that at the same time, he will never fall too low and will always be able to work with people of great worth that appreciate his talent. As a result, I think he is happy and feels safe. In *The Underneath*, he was synchronous with the kind of rhythm that I was looking for, and we shared the same sense of humor. Also, he's not afraid to appear unlikeable, which would not be the case for a big star. For the role of Rachel, I wanted someone who was not known to the public because I wanted people to think *a priori* that she was a jerk. The audience should not have a point of reference. Alison Elliott seemed just right in relation to Peter; the contrast between the two of them was appropriate. When I met her, she reminded me right away of Lauren Bacall: tall, poised, with an opacity that appealed to me and did not let on what she was thinking. I only regret not to have been able to explore her talents to their fullest potential, and have given her a narrow range. Adam Trese also struck me as a convincing brother for Peter. I always liked Joe Don Baker and I was happy to find a part for him. I wanted the secondary characters to be unknown to the audience, but the principals, except for Rachel, to be familiar actors. I was lucky that they all agreed, because we did not pay them much.

Q: *Your use of the subjective point of view in the hospital sequence is very striking.*
A: Our point of departure was the setting. We had five different types of windows, two different kinds of mirrors. The ceiling was on a pivot, which

enabled us to vary the angle in relation to the characters present in the room. There was a different color for each person, and little by little, the tones became warmer. When the mother arrives, there is no furniture, which we introduced progressively. It was not until we had set up the first shot with the mother, filmed at an angle, that I decided not to show Peter at all, which was not our intention at the start. We only see Peter once his brother is absent. I also wanted the dissolves to be shorter and shorter. At the beginning, with the mother, the dissolve was between 12 and 14 seconds; and at the end there were none. What also helped was that my director of photographer, Elliot Davis, was the cameraman as well. When the two detectives are there, you have the feeling that the gaze has suddenly been awaken for an instant from a sound sleep, then blinks again. Had we made a big budget film, I would have gotten calls from the studio wanting to know why we had no shots of Peter Gallagher's face. I like the transition from this subjective and extremely stylized shot to the shot of the man appearing in the hallway. He is awake and attentive, and the contrast is striking. We share his anxiety because we don't know who the intruder is.

Q: *What about Shelly Duvall?*
A: I always liked her. Also, the idea of someone who would be in a drug induced state, almost hallucinatory, and who finds coming out of it that the nurse is as strange as Shelly Duvall, appealed to me. It's really too much! I also wanted to hear her talk about Stanley Kubrick during the shooting of *The Shining;* between shots she would tell me some frightening anecdotes! But she did it with a lot of humor.

Q: *In the text you gave to* Projections Four, *you talked about one of your favorite films,* The Third Man, *and the words you used—disillusion, betrayal, misguided sexual desire—could also apply to your own films.*
A: And that's true also for *The Underneath;* I am incapable of knowing why. There is also a great sense of urban setting in *The Third Man,* with this city that will soon not be what it was at the end of the war. The great use of black and white. Of all the film noirs, I really like *Asphalt Jungle* and *Chinatown,* with its mix of classicism and modern sensibility; it's hard to do. Everything works to perfection: the setting, the actors, the staging, the cinematography. When Polanski is at his best, he is amazingly economical. When you think back on the film, you remember its density and complexity, and when you

watch it again, you are struck by its simplicity. The problem with many directors nowadays is that their complexity is superficial. That's easy. Polanski's staging of the action in *Chinatown* is the opposite: it comes from an understanding of and an experience with cinema that has nothing superficial about it.

Q : *For the first time, you were not responsible for the editing of* The Underneath.
A : Yes, because at the end of *King of the Hill,* I realized that writing, directing, and editing the film left me in such a state of exhaustion that after editing I made some wrong choices: I had lost all perspective. So I decided not to let myself fall into a similar situation for my next film, and I really enjoyed working with Stan Salfas. It was a luxury to have someone with whom to talk. But for my small budget films I will be my own editor again.

Soderbergh's *The Underneath* Brings '90s Style to Film Noir

KEVIN LALLY/1995

EVERYTHING CHANGED—ALL IN SOME WAYS, nothing
changed—for writer-director Steven Soderbergh with the unveiling of his
debut feature, *sex, lies, and videotape*, in 1989. A wry tale of a young man with
a penchant for taping women's intimate sexual confessions, the film was the
surprise winner of the Palme d'Or at Cannes and went on to become a major
indie box-office success. If he had wanted to, Soderbergh could have leapt
into any high-profile studio project he fancied. Instead, he's remained true
to the spirit of his breakthrough hit, steering an independent course with a
series of personal, modestly budgeted films that have allowed him to
broaden his palette. His second film, the expressionistic thriller *Kafka*, earned
mixed reviews, but his followup, *King of the Hill*, was one of the best-received
movies of 1993, an evocative coming-of-age story based on the memoirs of
author A. E. Hotchner.

With his new Gramercy release, *The Underneath*, Soderbergh combines the
stylistic daring of *Kafka* with the sharp insight into human relationships of
sex, lies. It may be his best film to date. A reworking of the 1949 Robert Siodmak *film noir Criss Cross, The Underneath* centers on Michael Chambers, a
handsome reformed gambler who returns to his home town of Austin, Texas
and finds himself drawn to his ex-wife Rachel, who is now involved with a
local gangster. Circumstances lead Michael into the biggest gamble of his
life: an armored-car heist which goes horribly awry.

Rather than construct a traditional *film noir*, Soderbergh has created what

From *Film Journal International*, May 1995. Reprinted by permission.

he calls "a relationship movie with a crime in the middle." Not only does he emphasize character over mayhem, but Soderbergh conceives his own style, with heightened use of primary colors, startling wide-screen compositions and eerily discordant soundtrack effects. Soderbergh's script (written under the pseudonym Sam Lowry—the hero of Terry Gilliam's *Brazil*—after a dispute with the Writers Guild over shared credit with the original film's writer, Daniel Fuchs) also has a sophisticated narrative structure, alternating among three different time frames. The superb cast includes *sex, lies* star Peter Gallagher as Michael, newcomer Alison Elliott in an attention-grabbing turn as the enigmatic Rachel, William Fichtner (TV's *Grace Under Fire*), Adam Trese (*Laws of Gravity*), Joe Don Baker, Paul Dooley, Elisabeth Shue and Anjanette Comer.

The Film Journal spoke to the 32-year-old filmmaker by phone at his home base in Baton Rouge, Louisiana.

F J : *Did you know the original film* Criss Cross *before you got involved with this project?*
s s : No, not until it was shown to me. Universal sent me a tape and said, "We've been thinking about trying to remake this—take a look at it and see if you'd be interested in being involved." I thought it was okay—I frankly didn't think it was a classic, and that was part of its appeal in terms of a remake. I thought there were some good ideas in it that I wanted to take a little further. And so I said, yeah, why don't we take a whack at this?

F J : *I like the way you take what is a typical* film noir *and totally reconceptualize it.*
s s : That's either going to be its saving or its downfall, I'm not sure which. Again, part of what attracted me to it was that the skeleton, in a sense, really lent itself to my preoccupations and it was very clear to me that there was plenty of opportunity for me to explore the issues that I generally like to explore—the idea of this guy coming back and trying to fix a relationship and, more importantly, the concept of a character being confused about the idea of something and the reality of something. I don't think Michael is able to delineate between the idea of putting the relationship with Rachel back together—and whether he's just enamored of that idea—and the reality of it. And I think she exploits that confusion. All that stuff I found potentially interesting.

Andie MacDowell and James Spader, *sex, lies, and videotape*, 1989

Jeremy Irons, *Kafka*, 1991

Jesse Bradford and Adrien Brody, *King of the Hill*, 1993

Jesse Bradford and Jeroen Krabbe, *King of the Hill*, 1993

Peter Gallagher and Alison Elliott, *The Underneath*, 1995

Jennifer Lopez and George Clooney, *Out of Sight*, 1998

George Clooney, *Out of Sight*, 1998

Terence Stamp and Luis Guzman, *The Limey*, 1999

Albert Finney and Julia Roberts, *Erin Brockovich*, 2000

Michael Douglas, *Traffic*, 2000

F J : *I think most* film noirs *are about relationships, but the people are archetypes. In this case, these are people you could see in your neighborhood bar.*

S S : Absolutely. Again, it remains to be seen whether or not that ended up being a good thing or a bad thing. That was certainly my intent, to ground the movie in some real behavior and real characters. As a result, the relationships and people's motives are somewhat more ambiguous. But I feel the best *noir* films, like *Chinatown* for instance, really have both going—they have characters that are realistic and a plot that keeps your attention. *Chinatown*'s a better plotted film than ours, by a long shot, but a lot of *noirs* tend to be too heavy on plot, at the expense of character. It's possible I went a little far in the other direction—but that's what interested me.

F J : *Did you have a personal set of guidelines as to certain genre things that you didn't want to do?*

S S : Yeah! No wet streets, no smoke, no hats, no long shadows. I wanted to avoid the traditional trappings of the genre, and at least shift them into another area. We tried to come up with the equivalent trappings, which in our case had more to do with the way we would stage things—color, framing, pictorial tonality, light and dark as opposed to just plain shadows. I didn't want it to look like a pastiche.

F J : *What does the title* The Underneath *mean to you?*

S S : For me, it means that a superficial reading of the movie and its plot are in a sense the least interesting aspects of the movie. To me, the really fun stuff is the subtext and what is unspoken. I didn't want to call the film *Criss Cross,* and I was just sitting down trying to come up with titles that (a) sounded interesting and didn't sound like everything else out there and (b) were also somewhat appropriate. That one just sort of stuck. It was fun to say and it just seemed to fit. Obviously there was a great fear on the part of Universal that people would think it was some aquatic adventure film, but I convinced them that people would see ads for the movie and there would be no danger of them thinking it was *Sea Hunt.*

F J : *I was reading a few of the interviews that appeared when* sex, lies, and video-tape *opened, and you were very frank about this bad patch in your personal life. It seems to me the Peter Gallagher character is an extension of all of that.*

ss: Yeah. I definitely thought that the film was a flip side of *sex, lies,* in the sense that I was never really happy with the ending of that film; I think in the long run it's probably a mistake to go back, and this was a way to rectify that in my own mind, to make something that I felt was a little more emotionally accurate. And also it was the opportunity to see what the relationship was beforehand—in *sex, lies,* there's this reference to this person from the past and we never really got to know what that relationship was about. This sort of provided the opportunity to show what he had left, what he was trying to correct. That was intriguing to me, and obviously represents the biggest difference between *The Underneath* and the original *Criss Cross,* in that you never saw what the characters' relationship was like before. I went through several different concepts of what that relationship was like until I settled on the one that's in the film. I tried out different sorts of addictions, different types of aberrant behavior, different structures. For a while—it was really confusing—the distant past was actually told in reverse order, and when I looked at a cut of the film like that it confused even people that were familiar with the film. I thought: That's a little too clever for its own good, so we straightened it out.

fj: *What kind of input did Peter Gallagher have into shaping his character?*
ss: A lot. A lot in the sense of me knowing Peter, me having written it with Peter in mind, and shading it to what I think he does well. In that sense, he was influencing it before he even knew it existed. I didn't call him until it was finished. And then once we started rehearsing, things came out of that. He and I just tend to have similar approaches and find similar things funny and similar things serious. It's a very easy, and at this point almost non-verbal, relationship. What's great about him is that he has no concern about whether something makes him look good or bad. At the end of the day, looking at the whole movie, I found it such a secure performance—it's so unmannered and un-actory. You need to be a very secure actor to do that. It's not a showy role—it's a complicated role, but not externally. He really resisted the urge to tart it up and make him more lively, because the whole point is that he was a lot more lively when he was gambling and drinking. That's the sad fact, that his life isn't as exciting, and that's probably what pulls him into this thing, the desire to feel that again.

F J : *He's such a charming guy that it adds to the ambiguity of the character.*

S S : Yeah, absolutely. That whole point that his brother makes that "you've really coasted on your looks and your charm"—I wanted to use Peter's looks to point out the fact that for somebody who looks like that, life can be a lot less demanding than for other people.

F J : *I've always wondered why he isn't a bigger star, but there's a real integrity to his career that's a lot more valuable than stardom.*

S S : I think so, too. He's always working, and he's always doing good work, more often than not in interesting films. At the end of the day, if Peter doesn't end up reaching the peaks of celebrity and fame that other actors reach, that may not be a bad thing. That may mean that he'll be around a lot longer and have a better career. He certainly seems content. He's read so many articles that have said, "This is the one that's going to make Peter a star," but he seems pretty pleased with the way things are going. He just likes to work.

F J : *Tell me how you found Alison Elliott.*

S S : Through the normal audition circuit. [Casting director] Ronnie Yeskel and I saw a lot of people, and Alison reminded me very much of a young Lauren Bacall, specifically in the sense that she was really hard to read sometimes. There was a smoky quality about her. We screen-tested her with Peter, and the two of them seemed to really hit it off. I was trying to make a point about Rachel's being somewhat opaque, and whether Michael's enamored of just the idea of this, or Rachel specifically. I wanted to make all that sort of fuzzy by making her hard to read. Alison was really good at that. You sense that there's something going on, that she's smart. At the same time, you wonder: God, why does she constantly pin her hopes to these men, especially *these* kinds of men? What's going on with her? And I wanted you to *not know* what was going on with her. Also, as you talked about, Alison looks like somebody who could be in your neighborhood—she's attractive, but she's not one of those movie femme fatale types. All of that, combined with the fact that I wanted somebody who was, as far as the public was concerned, an unknown, so that you wouldn't be thinking: Oh, I've seen her play this part, I bet she's going to go this way.

FJ: *This is your fourth film, and you've never made a traditionally commercial picture. Is it a struggle to keep making the kinds of films you want to make?*
SS: Not yet! It may be soon, but thus far it hasn't been a struggle at all. Believe me, I've got it great. I think it would be a tougher situation if I'd made films that were, from the ground up, designed to be more commercial and were more expensive and all that. I don't think any of the films I've made have carried with them the kinds of commercial expectations that a lot of other filmmakers have to deal with. So people look at *King of the Hill*—it didn't cost a lot of money, and I don't think they were saying, "My God, what a huge failure for him," because it just wasn't that kind of movie. I don't think anybody looked at it and thought it was going to be a block-buster. We all hoped it wouldn't lose money, but I don't think we had any illusions about how it was going to perform. But it's a strange time—I certainly wonder whether or not the movies I'm interested in making are movies that people are interested in seeing, over and above the exigencies of the timing of the movie's release and what else is out there and things that you can't control. The kinds of movies I grew up on in the late '60s and early '70s that I responded to, I don't know that people really want to go see those anymore.

FJ: *There seems to be a real schism right now. Studio commercial films have never been more crass, yet the independent film movement seems pretty strong.*
SS: It is in some cases. I just think it's all pretty blurry. It's just obvious to me that the A films of 20 and 25 years ago are now art films, and the B films are now the A films, from the studio's standpoint. So that leaves me sort of with one foot in and one foot out. But I can't really complain.

FJ: *I'm sure you've been asked this before, but after* sex, lies, and videotape, *did you have to go through some kind of decompression or recovery period from all the expectations surrounding you?*
SS: No, not really. It was disorienting, because it was so unexpected. But because it was unexpected, it made it easier to deal with. I knew that I hadn't asked for it, I hadn't campaigned for it. It's funny to read people bashing you for having won an award, say at Cannes, that you certainly did not ask for and did not expect. It wasn't *my* fault. I certainly knew that it was going to come back to me, in the sense that all this praise would be turned around at some point. But that's fine. If that's all I have to deal with, then that's pretty

easy. I don't live in Los Angeles, I'm not privy to the sort of discussions and parlor games about who's on top and who's not and who's a failure and who's a success. I don't hear it, so I don't really think about it that much. I just want to work. I think other people thought about it a lot more than I did.

Crazy for You: Steven Soderbergh Cuts Loose with *Schizopolis*

PATRICIA THOMSON/1996

SCHIZOPOLIS OPENS WITH A LONG SHOT of a manic crazy-man clad only in a tee-shirt fleeing across a green lawn with two men in white in hot pursuit. It's a situation the film's director, Steven Soderbergh, likens to being an independent filmmaker: "You want to be free, but everyone's trying to tackle you and bring you down."

With *Schizopolis,* Soderbergh refused to be wrestled into conformity. His fifth feature is an idiosyncratic, energetic, and blissfully uncommercial comedy that represents a complete departure from the director's expected career track—a screeching U-turn, in fact, that takes him back to the world of no-budget filmmaking. Shot over a 10-month period in Soderbergh's hometown of Baton Rouge, *Schizopolis* came together with the help of friends who took deferred salaries and sometimes doubled as crew and cast. For his part, Soderbergh not only wrote and directed the film, but also served as cinematographer and played two of the leads.

For indie directors who envy the kind of studio deals and comfortable budgets Soderbergh had previously managed to land, *Schizopolis* is a surprising career twist. But it's no fluke; the writer/director is already at work on a sequel.

As the whole world knows, Soderbergh made his remarkable debut in 1989 with *sex, lies & videotape,* which cost $1.2 million and grossed almost $25 million domestically after winning the Palme d'Or at Cannes and making it

From *The Independent Film and Video Monthly,* April 1997. Reprinted with permission of the author.

into multiplexes everywhere. Its critical and financial success marks a milestone in independent film history, launching the current chapter in which indie film is taken seriously by industry, audiences, and college career counselors. From there Soderbergh went on to direct *Kafka* (1991), produced by Barry Levinson and backed by French financiers to the tune of $11 million; Universal's *King of the Hill* (1993), made for $8 million; and the $6.5 million *The Underneath* (1995), also made with Universal. *Schizopolis,* in contrast, cost a mere $250,000—about one-fourth the budget of *sex, lies & videotape.*

Film-goers who have caught *Schizopolis* on the festival circuit have called it everything from "brilliant" to "the worst movie ever made." Filmmakers tend to love it, especially its freewheeling energy and wacky, witty film jokes that recall the cinematic shenanigans of Richard Lester (the subject of a book Soderbergh is writing), Monty Python, and the French New Wave. But critics thus far have tended to hold their heads and groan.

Schizopolis is a wild ride, to say the least, and it's giddy fun for those willing to lay back and let it happen. Bursting with an exuberant sense of experimentation, *Schizopolis* is loaded with verbal and visual jokes, bizarre non sequiturs, and goofy slapstick. While it sticks to a three-act structure (watch for the numbers), the plot careens like a drunken sailor between its story of double *doppelgangers,* involving a corporate-drone speechwriter for a New Age guru and a randy dentist (both played by Soderbergh), and their love interests (played by the director's ex-wife, Betsy Brantley). But beneath its jokey surface lie some more serious concerns: anxiety in the workplace, the loss of meaningful communication at home, and the vaporous content of New Age gurus who pretend to offer solutions to a society that's adrift and alienated.

Schizopolis was a tough sell to distributors, most of whom were stumped by the question of how to market such a feature. Northern Arts, a small but growing distributor based in Massachusetts, took up the challenge, picking up domestic theatrical rights. (Previous releases include *Drunks, Tokyo Decadence, I Just Wasn't Made for These Times, Wallace & Gromit: A Close Shave* and *The Best of Aardman,* and *Chameleon Street.*) Fox Lorber has domestic video rights and will handle world sales. *Schizopolis* opens in theaters this month.

The Independent caught up with Soderbergh at the Toronto and Hamptons film festivals, where he was presenting both his film of a Spalding Gray monologue, *Gray's Anatomy* (an Independent Film Channel commission), and the surreal, irrepressible *Schizopolis.*

Q: *Let's begin with the genesis of* Schizopolis. *How long were the ideas for the various strands floating around—the* doppelganger *theme, the New Age religion, your play on the language of cinema—and when did they coalesce? Or did the idea for the film come as a piece?*

A: It was a little bit of everything. Some of the ideas I'd been carrying around for a long time. Some were discovered when I began to write the screenplay. Others happened while we were shooting.

Q: *How did the pseudo-Scientology theme, here called "Eventualism," develop?*

A: It grew out of my interest in gurus and people's desire to find a way to order their lives in a world they're finding increasingly hostile and complicated. I'm always fascinated when people relinquish control of their lives to someone else, especially a stranger. That's always struck me as odd.

I didn't really have Scientology in mind specifically. I don't find Scientology stranger than any religion. Personally, I find them all weird. But Scientology is one of the few religions that advertises on television and has images that are instantly recognizable that I could appropriate—the volcano, the book. You see that image and it conjures up something.

Q: *And it's not the Methodist Church.*

A: Right. So there was that and also it played into the idea of paranoia and in-fighting within a company. That sort of thing tends to be more pronounced in an organization that is run by one very mercurial personality.

Q: *Have you ever worked at a place like that?*

A: Sure. When I was doing odd jobs, I worked for companies that were basically run by autocrats and they were very unpredictable. Your life hung in the balance seemingly every half-hour.

Q: *You play the two main characters: Fletcher Munson, the speech-writer for the New Age guru, and a dentist who has an affair with Munson's wife. I saw these characters as two different people. But when the dentist says, "I'm having an affair with my own wife," that throws that interpretation into a tailspin. What's that line about?*

A: Well, basically what's happened is he's jumped rails onto somebody else's life, but is aware of that. So when he realizes "I've jumped into somebody's else's life" and it turns out that somebody was having an affair with his wife, he's a little freaked out by that, as anybody would be.

So in the part of the film with Fletcher Munson, which takes place over the course of two or three days, when he jumps ship to this other life, he has been reliving those two or three days as the dentist—sort of skipping backwards. Then in the third act we see those days from [the wife's] perspective. That grew out of my interest in parallel time structures.

Q: *Where did the two main characters come from? They're off the beaten track, and I doubt they came from your immediate sphere....*
A: Oh, sure, why wouldn't they be? I've seen a lot of dentists.

Q: *Reaching that age where your fillings fall out?*
A: No, I've just had a long history of correction and bullshit. I actually have come into contact with a *lot* of dentists. So I picked a profession and a type I thought I knew well.

But the idea of *doppelgangers*, parallel universes, and parallel time frames is something that's always interested me. I had an idea to do something about that for several years. But it wasn't until I was making *The Underneath* that I decided it was time to change what I was doing and how I was doing it. Sort of start over again.

Q: *In terms of what? The scale of production? Narrative structure?*
A: Everything. Just start over again. Rediscover the joy of filmmaking, which I'd slowly begun to lose over the course of the four films I directed.

Q: *Why was that?*
A: I don't know. I was just drifting off course. I'm sure there are tons of reasons, some personal and some professional. The bottom line was I sort of woke up in the middle of *The Underneath* and felt I was making a movie I wasn't interested in. When I began to question whether or not I wanted to make movies anymore, I realized that what I needed to do was change what I was doing.

So it's a progression, in a weird sort of way. Even though *The Underneath* is my least favorite, in retrospect it may have been my most important film, because the dissatisfaction drove me into a new area.

Q: *Is this direction related to your earlier shorts?*
A: The shorts I made were very similar.

Q: *In what respect?*
A: Energy, comic stance.

Q: *When watching* Schizopolis, *if you're into the humor—and some people weren't . . .*
A: How could you not *be?*

Q: *Well, some people really weren't—the overall feeling is that you're simply having a lark, that you yourself weren't taking the film too seriously.*
A: I needed a lark. *Schizopolis* is extreme in one way, and I think what will happen is I'll end up applying a lot of the things that I got out of *Schizopolis* to something a little less schizophrenic in terms of its story. The follow-up to *Schizopolis* that I'm getting ready to write is going to have the same energy, be made in the same way, and have the same m.o., but be a bit of a more linear story and not quite so complicated.

This thing, I just had to get a lot of it out of my system. Now I think I can see a balance between *Schizopolis* and a "normal" movie, whatever that is. I'm hoping I can apply some of what I've learned making *Schizopolis* to that film—just a way of working that is interesting and allows me more freedom.

Q: *Freedom in terms of what specifically?*
A: Stripping the crew down, getting rid of things that have been getting in the way, both from a technical standpoint and a practical crew standpoint. Things like video assist. You know, we made *Gray's Anatomy* with a crew of about a dozen, when it came right down to it. *Meet the Parents* [Soderbergh's remake of a low-budget first feature by Chicagoan Greg Gliana, which is now in development] could easily be made with a crew that size. A lot of things like that—operating the camera myself, trying to strip it down. I've decided that anybody who's not actively involved in what's going on in front of the camera needs to be eliminated, that somebody who's just standing there is an energy vacuum.

Q: *What kinds of changes did this freedom and flexibility allow you to make to the* Schizopolis *script during production?*

A: Sometimes you couldn't do what you thought you'd be able to do from a practical standpoint. You'd sit around—there'd be the four of us, or the five of us, if we were lucky—and say, "Hmm, I just don't think this is working." You'd go eat lunch and talk about why it wasn't working. And you'd drive around, see another location, and think, "Maybe the problem is location." You know, it was all very loose and informal, and it was strictly based on, do you feel it at the time? Do you feel like it's really happening? If it's not, let's not do it, and let's figure out why.

Q: *Did that create structural changes?*
A: Sometimes; not major ones. But some of the best things in the film resulted from either accidents or problems that were turned into advantages.

One of my favorite scenes is where [Eventualism guru T. Azimuth] Schwitters is going down the list of people who sent him condolences [for an assassination attempt]. In the script it's a scene between him and his wife. Well, the actress who played the wife had left town and not told anyone [he laughs]. So I said, "Does anybody know a girl in her early twenties who we could use to play his assistant?" Somebody goes off to make the phone call. In the meantime, I sit down and think, "Alright, here's the scene: They're in there, the right-hand man is pacing and she's reading out this list." We wrote the list right there. The girl showed up, we gave her the note pad, and we shot it. It's one of my favorite things in the movie.

The whole movie was like that. The analogy in sports would be when you're in the zone. I just felt in the zone all the time. I just felt [snapping his fingers] every decision was the right decision. Things just would fall into place, even when mistakes occurred.

Q: *Did* Schizopolis *come together in a substantial way in the editing stage?*
A: There's a lot of stuff we cut out of it, but I'd say the biggest changes were during shooting, just things that would occur to me. We started cutting while we were still shooting, so I was able to see if I needed things.

The great thing about it being a movie made by just a handful of people with your own equipment was we literally could sit in the editing room and say, for instance, "We need a shot of an airplane landing" and go to the office, get the equipment, and go shoot an airplane. So the amount of time between idea and execution was very small. It was great.

Q : *Who were the other five people?*
A : John Hardy, my producer. David Jensen, who's a grip and also an actor; he plays Elmo Oxygen; he's worked on all my movies. Paul Ledford, who's my production sound mixer, also worked on all my movies. Mike Malone, who played Schwitters, was an on-set dresser in *The Underneath;* he was there for a large part of the shoot. And then there was usually a sort of rotating fifth person.

Q : *Several of the main themes in* Schizopolis *were also present in* sex, lies, and videotape, *namely the problem of communication between couples and the difficulty of marriage. Are these both personal films?*
A : Oh, sure. *Schizopolis* more so, despite its abstract, surreal quality; it's a closer representation of my experience of the difficulties in maintaining communications in a relationship than *sex, lies* was. It's all tied in together [with] what I see as the gradual simplification and almost destruction of our language. We've gotten lazy with it, and it's used to obscure instead of illuminate. So the struggle to keep life meaningful is getting more and more difficult.

Q : *Tell me about the scenes in the bathroom, when you're making faces in the mirror and masturbating in the stall. What was your intent?*
A : Well, you know, all that is intended to be amusing—the guy's chronic masturbation and all that—but what it means to me is not so funny. And that is, the culture, in the States especially, is so noisy and so overwhelming, and the forces that divide you from other people and from your community are so strong. The Me period that everybody went through yielded so little. I think the end result of all these things is a guy sitting there by himself looking in the mirror like that. This is where it's all leading if we're not careful—that specific type of emptiness.

I'd rather people laugh at it. But a couple of people have picked up on that, who said, "That stuff was really funny, but at the same time it was really sad."

That was a one-taker, you know. I just sort of did it.

Q : *I've been hearing a lot of positive word of mouth about your acting in* Schizopolis. *Is this something you would like to do again?*

A: Well, it wasn't acting. Those are just variations on my personality. It wasn't really a performance, as far as I was concerned. When there are four or five of you, and I'm lighting it and setting the shot, I go from behind the camera, then I walk and sit in the chair in front of the camera, and we roll. The whole thing was so fluid that you never really thought about it. Which is great! I don't know if I'd be that comfortable under the conditions that movies are normally made under. I don't really have any desire to find out.

Q: *Could you walk through the stages of financing* Schizopolis?
A: What happened was I called Universal during *The Underneath* and said, "I'm going to make this movie; I don't have a script. It's a comedy and it's in color, but that's all I know. I want you to buy North American video for 75 grand right now." And they did.

Then after we finished shooting, I said, "Look, I want to do another film like this, and I also need more money to finish *Schizopolis*. So for the second film, I'll sell you North American video and theatrical for $400,000 and you get the two films for $475,000"—always with the agreement that I could buy those rights back in order to get a distribution deal, which is what we ended up doing. When Fox Lorber came in, I used the money that Fox Lorber was paying to buy back the video rights for *Schizopolis*.

So at the end of the day, *Schizopolis* will end up costing about $250–$275,000, and with the remaining money, we'll make the sequel.

Q: *So Universal is handling nothing, and they've been paid back . . .*
A: They've been paid back for *Schizopolis*. They did it as a favor for me.

Q: *Did they take first look for theatrical?*
A: I think they knew. I told them, "You're not going to want this movie. This is just to keep me going." You know, I've had a good experience there. I made two movies there that didn't make them any money, and they've left me completely alone and still would like me to make a film there.

Q: *Are they asking to see the sequel's script?*
A: No. For them, this amount of money is infinitesimal. They pay that amount for writers to do a couple months of work on a script.

Q: *What else were you doing during the 10 months of off-and-on production?*

A: Writing scripts for other people, and then, late in *Schizopolis,* we started making *Gray's Anatomy.* So it was a pretty busy time.

Q: *What other scripts?*
A: One of them was *Nightwatch,* a Miramax film. I did some work on *Mimic,* which is shooting [in Toronto] now, although I don't think much of my work survived. I just turned in a draft of a script I'm writing for Henry Selleck [*James and the Giant Peach*], so I've been writing for hire back to back during the production of both films.

Q: *Do you see this as a way of continuing the new low-budget, stripped-down direction you're taking?*
A: Yeah, because I haven't taken a salary on a movie since I finished *The Underneath* in November of '94, so it's my only source of income. But I don't enjoy it, because I don't like to write. It's been hard, but it's my only option. I don't want to go direct for money, because it's too hard and it's a year-and-a-half. And commercials don't interest me.

Q: *In 10 Feet in 10 Days, Marina Zenovich's documentary-in-progress about Slam-dance, you state: "Independent films are creeping towards the mainstream, and I feel there needs to be another wave of really outrageously independent films. . . . People are not feeling as independent as they used to . . . because [they] are thinking they can make money. That's what people who make studio movies think. It's gotten to the point where people, before they're making their films, are wondering, 'Is this the kind of film that's going to get into Sundance?' As soon as that happens, it's really over. That's not what you're supposed to have in your head."*
Do you believe independent film is seriously off-course?
A: Maybe parts of it are, but there's always going to be someone who's not. I don't worry about interesting films getting made; I worry about how they're going to get seen. Because as the stakes get higher and it gets more and more expensive to release a movie, the distributors are going to be less willing to take a risk.

That's what I found. It was a frustrating summer, toting *Gray's Anatomy* and *Schizopolis* around and having everybody say, "I don't think we can make this work." We had one company say, "We ran the numbers and we decided that we actually could turn a profit with this film, but not enough of a profit to make it worth our time." And I thought, "Gee, if you can say that about all 12 films you release this year, that's a good year."

It was interesting both on *Schizopolis* and *Gray's* to reimmerse myself in an area I hadn't been in since *sex, lies,* which is the "We've made a film, now what do we do with it?" arena. It's changed. Yeah, getting the movie made is only half of it.

Suddenly Soderbergh: The Onetime Wunderkind Beats the Backlash

PAULA S. BERNSTEIN/1997

GENERIC BUT CATCHY INTRO. Meet at blah-blah hotel for lunch. Initial superficial response to subject's appearance. Unnecessary description of food subject has ordered. Inappropriate but shocking revelation about subject's childhood. Requisite witty quotes to promote subject's new films.

You know the drill and so does Steven Soderbergh. Since *sex, lies, and videotape* earned him international recognition in 1989 (the $1.2 million feature ended up grossing almost $100 million worldwide), the onetime wunderkind has been interviewed so many times that he could knock off a fill-in-the-blank celebrity profile about himself in minutes flat.

But, no doubt, it's more fun for the 34-year-old auteur to read journalists' off-the-cuff pop-psych diagnoses of his character and his once promising career. (Last month, the *L.A. Times Magazine* published an incisive expose entitled "The Funk of Steven Soderbergh" and, as the director points, out, "they did not mean funk as in George Clinton.")

Does he fear success? Is he purposely trying to piss off Hollywood? Doe he subconsciously want to be punished? It's easy to hypothesize about why Soderbergh's cinematic escapades post-*sex, lies* have flopped. But it's unfair and perhaps incorrect to dub Soderbergh a "failure" as many peers and critics have over the past eight years. How many failed directors complete six films in eight years? What other relative newcomer to Tinseltown has been able to make a pensive film about the life of Franz Kafka (*Kafka*) or a dark drama

From *Village Voice*, April 1, 1997. Reprinted with permission of the author.

about a young kid fending for himself during the Depression (*King of the Hill*), both on Hollywood studio tabs?

"My definition of success," says the director, who is handsome in a goofy, balding, lovable-geek sort of way, "is being able to do the work that you want to do. . . . I've never done anything because of how it would look. I've never not done anything because of how it would look. It's all about what I feel I need to do right now." About his first success, he says: "For whatever reason, people were interested in seeing that film at that time. It's like a Nehru jacket to me. It feels so of that particular time. It's almost a period piece. We didn't even think it would get released. So when Miramax came in [at the U.S. Film Festival, now Sundance] with an offer of $1 million, I felt bad for them. I thought, 'They're insane, they're throwing their money away. But we'll take it.' "

Longtime colleague Nancy Tenenbaum, who executive produced *sex, lies, and videotape* and recently worked with Soderbergh on Greg Mottola's *Daytrippers*, is tired of hearing industry peers criticize the filmmaker's unconventional career choices. "What a hard time these past years have been, to have everyone saying, 'His career is over' after *sex, lies.* 'It's over' after *Kafka.* Even people in his own camp would think, 'What's wrong with him? Why is he making *The Underneath?*' But he's evolving. He's constantly learning. He's constantly pushing himself to cover areas he hasn't done."

But after being singed by Hollywood (he is currently in litigation with Paramount Pictures and Scott Rudin over a planned adaptation of *A Confederacy of Dunces,* and had a falling out with former mentor Robert Redford over *King of the Hill*), Soderbergh skulked into a creative rut on the set of his fourth film, *The Underneath,* a contemporary noir. Feeling the need for a refresher course in the joys of indie filmmaking, he trekked down to his hometown of Baton Rouge, Louisiana, to shoot the experimental *Schizopolis* for $250,000.

Inspired by the Dadaist and Surrealist artists as well as by the eclectic triumvirate of Richard Lester, Luis Buñuel, and Monty Python, *Schizopolis,* which will open next month in New York, is a cynical yet reluctantly optimistic comedy.

"Generic greeting!" calls out Soderbergh's character Fletcher Munson as he arrives home to his doting wife and daughter in an early scene. "Generic greeting returned," his wife responds, blandly cheerful. A sly commentary on the cookie-cutter scripts being made into movies ("Certainly *Twister* would have worked with that kind of language," he says), the idea "grew out of what happens when a marriage has decayed to the point where language is rendered meaningless."

Though he can spew intellectual bullshit as well as the next self-educated indie director, Soderbergh also delights in cutting through the crap. Expounding on *Schizopolis* as a "provocation of sorts and a piece of agit-prop," a moment later he notes with pride that it could also be seen as an homage to "lowbrow variety-sketch movies like *The Groove Tube* and *Kentucky Fried Movie.* I love those movies."

But people who are close to Soderbergh see a far more personal subtext in *Schizopolis.* In fact, by casting his ex-wife (actress Betsy Brantley) and their young daughter as his family in the film, Soderbergh seem intent on drawing audiences to a potentially sore spot.

When asked what it was like directing and acting opposite his ex-wife, an unruffled Soderbergh deadpans, "I highly recommend it." Prodded to get into more detail about the unusual circumstances, he explains, "I think everybody must have thought I was insane while we were making the movie. But, then you think, 'It's just life. Why shy away from it?' In terms of my work, I'm always looking for the stupid thing to do, the thing that makes you think, 'Why would anybody put themselves through that?' It was very therapeutic. It really was like standing on the bow of a ship in a bad storm. It required an enormous amount of equilibrium."

After weathering *Schizopolis* Soderbergh extended his stay in Baton Rouge long enough to film Spalding Gray's monologue *Gray's Anatomy,* which opened last week at Film Forum. "So many of the ideas that are in *Gray's Anatomy* I would never have thought of or considered seriously had I not made *Schizopolis.* It is a willingness to drop everything and go after the better idea when it presents itself. That comes from security."

Ironically, filming the two low-budget movies back-to-back inspired the newly energized filmmaker to return to Hollywood. "I feel completely reinvigorated about making movies again which I was in danger of losing," he explains. Soderbergh cowrote the screenplay of the soon-to-be-released Ewan McGregor thriller *Nightwatch* and is currently producing *Pleasantville,* by first-time filmmaker Gary Ross. He's also editing a book of interviews with Richard Lester, one of his idols.

Recently, Soderbergh signed on to direct a screen adaptation of Elmore Leonard's *Out of Sight* for Universal Pictures, the same studio that barely broke even on *King of the Hill* and *The Underneath.*

But though George Clooney will star in *Out of Sight* Soderbergh is by no means selling out. The director insists that he just wants to make movies that people will see. In fact, because he realizes that *Schizopolis* may be "too dense and too complicated" Soderbergh tacked on a viewer-friendly prologue to ease the audience into the unconventional film: "In the event that you find certain sequences or ideas confusing," announces a soothing, monotoned Soderbergh trapped by a spotlight at microphone, "please bear in mind that this is your fault, not ours. You will need to see the picture again and again until you understand everything." Final clever remarks. Convenient and glib conclusion. Subject leaves the room.

Out of Sight

ED KELLEHER/1998

FILMMAKER STEVEN SODERBERGH ARRIVED on the interna-
tional cinema scene at the tender age of 26 in 1989, when his debut feature
sex, lies, and videotape captured the Palme d'Or at Cannes. Soderbergh followed that witty tale of obsession and betrayal with *Kafka* (1991), a fantasy
exploring the dark world of the renowned Czech writer. *King of the Hill* (1993),
based on a memoir by A. E. Hotchner, was an unsettling study of a 12-year-
old boy abandoned in a St. Louis hotel during the Great Depression. Next up
for Soderbergh was *The Underneath* (1993), a stylish revamping of the 1949 *film
noir, Criss Cross,* followed by a pair of low-budget efforts, *Gray's Anatomy*
(1996), featuring performance artist Spalding Gray, and, in the same year, the
little-seen but intriguing *Schizopolis.*

Now, Soderbergh takes a decisive step into the arena of mainstream mov-
ies via *Out of Sight,* a rowdy, violent crime-caper movie starring George
Clooney as a career bank robber who breaks out of prison, and Jennifer Lopez
as a federal marshal who falls in love with him. Ving Rhames (*Pulp Fiction*),
Albert Brooks (*Mother*), Don Cheadle (*Boogie Nights*) and Dennis Farina (*Get
Shorty*) co-star in the film, which boasts a screenplay by Scott Frank (*Get
Shorty*), adapted from an Elmore Leonard novel. Danny DeVito, Michael
Shamberg and Stacey Sher, partners in Jersey Films, produced the picture,
with Barry Sonnenfeld (*Men in Black*) and John Hardy (*sex, lies, and videotape,
The Underneath*) aboard as executive producers. Universal will release the film

From *Film Journal International,* June 1998. Reprinted by permission.

nationally on June 26. *Film Journal International* spoke with Soderbergh via telephone in early May.

FILM JOURNAL INTERNATIONAL: *The last time we talked was in 1989. You were calling from Gunnison, Colorado, to talk about* sex, lies.
STEVEN SODERBERGH: You were one of the people I called from the road.

FJI: *I remember thinking: This guy just won Cannes, he is under pressure, but he'll be able to handle it. Did you feel that way at the time?*
SS: It certainly didn't seem like the hardest thing in the world to sort out. There are worse problems to have.

FJI: *Still, there was a lot of focus on you.*
SS: Only in retrospect do I imagine that there was, because I see other people go through it now. At the time, it didn't really seem that intense.

FJI: *You've made a wide range of films since then, pictures that show your versatility. Was part of that to move away from* sex, lies?
SS: No, not specifically. It only reflected my eclecticism and my desire to try different things. I didn't feel formed yet. I still felt like I was very early on in my development. I wanted to experiment and try different things. That's the only thing I had in mind.

FJI: *After Cannes, you said it seemed like there was nowhere to go but downhill, yet you didn't go downhill . . .*
SS: Well, I went sideways, basically. Certainly, what I meant was that the odds of my being the focus of such unified positive attention again were probably pretty slim. It just doesn't happen very often to people and it certainly doesn't happen very often to your first film.

FJI: *Let's talk about* Out of Sight. *How did you get involved? Were you a fan of Elmore Leonard?*
SS: I had read a half-dozen of his books, had seen a half-dozen or so of the movies based on some of his books, and liked him. I got a call from Casey Silver [chairman] at Universal, who I've known for a long time, actually, and who I dealt with on two movies before. He said: "Look, we've got the script over here and Jersey Films is trying to find a director and I think you're going

to like this script and you should go in and talk to them." So they sent me the script and I read it and it was a terrific script. Clooney was attached at that point and I thought he'd be great in it. And I told them: "Jersey is great, they're smart producers and I like you guys at the studio, and this is the kind of material I do well—and I don't want to do it."

F J I : *Why not?*
S S : Mostly because, at the time, I had something else I was trying to get off the ground. Casey said: "Don't be an idiot, the odds of the planets lining up like this are so small that you really should pursue this." I realized he was right, so I did pursue it. I went and basically auditioned for Jersey and Clooney a couple of times and got the job.

F J I : *Did it bother you, or did it cross your mind, that the subject matter of* Out of Sight *was somewhat Tarantino-esque?*
S S : Not to me, the way I saw the movie. I felt that its tone and its approach would be very different from his, because we're very different people and very different filmmakers. When you look at [Barry Sonnenfeld's] *Get Shorty* and *Jackie Brown* and *Out of Sight,* it's a nice lesson in what a director does to a piece of material, how a director filters material through his or her goggles, and makes it something specific. So I wasn't worried about that. I think Tarantino's influence has been so significant that people forget he was influenced by other people who came before him, in terms of style and tone and structure of storytelling. These things have been around. It just so happens that none of [the films that influenced Tarantino] made a hundred million dollars and sort of invaded the culture to the degree that *Pulp Fiction* did. So I wasn't really worried about that. It didn't even occur to me. I knew he was preparing *Jackie Brown,* but I also knew that it was probably going to be a very different movie than the one I wanted to make.

F J I : Out of Sight *certainly has a great "meet-cute" scene, with George Clooney and Jennifer Lopez squeezed together in the trunk of a getaway car. Was that your idea?*
S S : It was in the book. It's pretty bizarre. I shot it twice, actually. I shot it wrong the first time. Then I went back and shot it again, and took the opportunity, while we were doing it, for Scott Frank to tweak it a little bit, writing-wise. It's a tough scene, in a way, because it's very important and it's odd,

and initially it was very long. It's shorter now. It was the subject of much discussion on the film, certainly.

F J I : *It's a movie that starts right in, and just goes. It's a fast-moving film.*
S S : It's about ten minutes shorter now, so I think it's moving even better. When I went in to meet with Jersey and Clooney, I said that I saw it as a combination of an early William Friedkin movie and a Hal Ashby movie. It should have the energy of a Friedkin movie from the '70s, but its approach to character and its balance of drama and humor should be like Ashby, and everybody immediately knew what I was talking about.

F J I : *What are your strengths as a filmmaker?*
S S : That's a tough question to answer without seeming to be self-aggrandizing. I like actors. I feel comfortable with them. When you hire good ones, they have great ideas and things happen that are unexpected and interesting and entertaining, and I like that process a lot. In terms of style, there are two ways of working. There are directors who have a signature style and they look for material they can impose that style on. Then there are filmmakers who work from the material outward and who ask what kind of style is appropriate for this material. I'm the second kind. I'm not assuming anything, stylistically, when I open a script, but as I read on, I might have an instinct about what kind of style is appropriate for this movie. But *Out of Sight*, stylistically, doesn't feel like *King of the Hill* or *The Underneath*. It's got a different vibe to it, and it's one that I thought was appropriate to that material. It's a little rougher around the edges.

F J I : The Underneath *was a strange, hypnotic movie that never found its audience.*
S S : It was made at a time when I was having great difficulty figuring out where I was going, creatively. I was not rigorous enough with that film. It should have been ripped apart and put back together in a more interesting way, conceptually. It should have been funnier. It was too somber, too serious. What it did, though, was drive me to start over again and go and make *Schizopolis* and *Gray's Anatomy* in a sort of amateur fashion and reawaken my interest and excitement about making movies, which, during *The Underneath* was in danger of being extinguished. That was a very scary thing, because I don't know how to do anything else.

F J I : *Is that kind of reawakening something you're likely to do again in the future?*
S S : It depends. I think I unlocked something. I don't feel in danger of making a movie that, for me, is hermetically sealed the way *The Underneath* was and the way *Kafka* is, to a large extent. I think I've gotten through that. Frankly, I think I just had a bad case of the 20s.

F J I : *At the time of* sex, lies, *you said that your initial instinct back then was to shoot in black-and-white, which probably, in retrospect, would not have been such a good idea.*
S S : A huge mistake. A fatal mistake. But a common youthful wish. What's important is to tap into the passion and excitement that you have when you're young and starting out, but take advantage of your knowledge of the world and of filmmaking to put that energy across in a way that's more mature. You know, this is a process. What's most disconcerting about the business now is how difficult it is to learn and grow and make mistakes. I'm lucky in that all the mistakes I've made up to this point have happened in a very small arena and, as such, have not been held against me. Nobody considers *The Underneath* to be a bomb, even though it lost almost all of its money, because it didn't cost very much and nobody expected it to make a lot of money. So I don't get nailed the way a lot of people do. But it's very difficult to have your head up the ass of Hollywood and keep doing what you want to do. There's a lot of pressures, both seen and unseen, to bring you into line. It's not for the faint of heart.

F J I : *Observers tend to think of a career as something that a filmmaker sees in the future, but one doesn't really know what that career is until much later.*
S S : Exactly. The problem is that now people see a career as being 18 months. I was, from the beginning, thinking: I want John Huston's career. I want a lot of movies over a long period of time. And then we'll go back, if we want to—I don't want to, but somebody else can—and sort it all out. . . . You need to plug in every once in a while to the thing that made you want to do it in the first place, because it's so easy to get cut off from that. I worked very hard to keep myself separate from the parts of this business that I think are destructive, at worst, and distracting, at best.

F J I : *What's your next project?*

s s : I'm developing a film based on a TV series called *Traffik* that ran in Britain about ten years ago. It's about how drugs move, how the drug business works, from beginning to end. That show was really terrific. It had four separate stories that it tracked in parallel time, and occasionally they intersected. It's just a fascinating look at how drugs move. It seems like a ripe time to make a movie about that in this country, especially with the complexity of our relationship with Mexico. I want to make it like [Costa-Gavras'] *Z*. I want it to be a fast-paced run-and-gun movie about how this stuff works.

Sight Seeing: Steven Soderbergh Loosens Up

DENNIS LIM/1998

STEVEN SODERBERG DOESN'T THINK MUCH of the widely circulated theory that *Out of Sight* is his comeback movie. "What's that Gloria Swanson line from *Sunset Boulevard?* 'I hate that word. It's a return!' I guess my question would be 'Back from what?' I've been pretty busy."

Busy reinventing himself, to be exact. After his last studio picture, 1995's ambitious but confused noir update *The Underneath* Soderbergh retreated to his hometown of Baton Rouge, Louisiana, and, guerrilla-style, knocked out a couple of no-budget films, the Spalding Gray monologue *Gray's Anatomy* and *Schizopolis*, a brilliant and seriously unhinged psychodrama that combined baffling semiotic games with lowbrow sketch comedy ("I thought it might end up with a small, disturbed following," he says). Not the most obvious preparation for an Elmore Leonard adaptation—George Clooney vehicle, but the director insists, "Those films really loosened me up. *Schizopolis* in particular taught me the value of not dissecting things ahead of time." As faithful as it remains to the source material, *Out of Sight* is unmistakably Soderbergh's movie, filled with small personalizing touches. "I guess it was self-evident to everybody that if I did it, there was no way I wasn't going to pee on it," he says. "It was going to have my stench no matter what. Fortunately, that's what they wanted. Jersey Films made it clear that they had no desire to make *Get Shorty 2.*

"The trick was finding that balance between not fucking it up and staying loose," he says. "*Schizopolis* was the most fun I'd ever had making a movie—

From *Village Voice*, June 7, 1998. Reprinted by permission.

running around with five friends, shooting whatever the hell you want, nothing can top that—but I'd say *Out of Sight* was the most fun you could have making a studio movie."

Asked what the new film has in common with his earlier, decidedly more sober work, he replies, "At the end of the day, it's slightly fatalistic. And thanks to Elmore Leonard, there's a very nonreductive view of people. I like that the characters don't change. I don't see that happening in life very much, so I tend to be suspicious when people undergo big changes in films."

Famously good with actors, Soderbergh refuses to take too much credit for the revelatory lead performances in *Out of Sight* or for the wonderfully vivid supporting ones. "George came in knowing exactly what he needed to do. He got it right and I didn't fuck with it. And if you look at the cast, these are people who know what they're doing." If *Out of Sight* feels like the kind of film that gets every last detail right, it has much to do with his collaborators, Soderbergh says, citing Elliot Davis's "space- and color-conscious" cinematography and the "hilarious" score by Belfast DJ David Holmes ("I wanted a combination of Lalo Schifrin's *Dirty Harry* and the first year of *The Rockford Files,* and David just totally got it").

A long-germinating Soderbergh project, an adaptation of *A Confederacy of Dunces,* is now back with him after a legal battle with producer Scott Rudin. He's also about to start work on an original screenplay, "something with the narrative spine of *sex, lies and videotape,* but the modus operandi of *Schizopolis.*"

At the end of the interview, Soderbergh says, "Do you think people have given up trying to figure me out?" The official line, I tell him, is that he's unpredictable and uncategorizable. "Good," he says. "I knew if I kept going that would happen after a while."

Back in Sight: The Return of Steven Soderbergh

PAUL MALCOLM/1998

A FEW MONTHS BACK, while Steven Soderbergh was in the thick of postproduction on his latest film, *Out of Sight,* his past caught up with him, again. *Sex, lies, and videotape* was being remastered for DVD, and Soderbergh, who had to oversee the process, says it was the first time he'd seen his 1989 feature debut in the nine years since its initial release. *Sex, lies* is, of course, the film that won the then-26-year-old director the Palme d'Or at Cannes, and, with its phenomenal commercial success, ushered in the Age of Sundance, when first-time filmmakers could become overnight celebrities. "It was really disorienting," Soderbergh says about revisiting the film. "It was the first time I'd been able to watch it and feel like somebody else had made it, and that's the result of how busy I've been."

Soderbergh has been busy, it's just that hardly anyone has noticed. In the years since his first feature, he has directed six films and executive-produced three more (*Suture, The Daytrippers* and the upcoming *Pleasantville*), but he's still largely pigeonholed as the guy who made *sex, lies*—largely because it's the only one of his movies that earned any money. "In retrospect, I think that's the most memorable thing about it," says the notoriously self-critical Soderbergh, shifting broadly in the chair of his tiny, cluttered office on the Universal lot, a *Repulsion* poster looming on the wall behind him. With more than a little frustration in his voice, he adds, "It's time for me to get a new middle name."

Which is probably one reason why Soderbergh has made the new George

From *LA Weekly,* July 3, 1998. Reprinted by permission.

Clooney movie. In *Out of Sight,* the indie hero whose films nobody goes to see has found a high-profile Hollywood project that could garner him the largest audience of his career. But coming hot on the heels of *Get Shorty* and *Jackie Brown,* the Elmore Leonard adaptation starring Clooney and Jennifer Lopez seems, for Soderbergh, like a particularly uncharacteristic capitulation to industry trends. He is, after all, the man who used the heat off of *sex, lies* to make *Kafka.*

Still, no one should cry sellout just yet: Soderbergh has already sunk his studio-size salary from the film into getting his long-languishing plans for *A Confederacy of Dunces* off the ground. (He regained the rights to John K. Toole's cult novel in the fall of 1997 after winning his lawsuit against Paramount, which had appropriated them from him.) Even more significantly, Soderbergh says he approached *Out of Sight* as the continuation of a creative rebirth that began several years back.

"I felt like I was at the end of my career four films in, that's how lethargic I felt," he says of his experience directing *The Underneath,* a neo-noir he shot in 1995. "I was really drifting into a place that wasn't very interesting, it wasn't very challenging. And that happens. It's all part of the process you go through when you're trying to figure out what it is you're good at and what you ought to be doing."

To break through the stagnation, Soderbergh put his own money into the screwball, stylistic freak-out that is *Schizopolis* (1997). With its pointed disdain for narrative coherence and its emphasis on sheer momentum, the movie unfolds like it's spilling straight out of the director's head. It's a sharp departure from the meticulous craftsmanship of *Kafka, King of the Hill* and *The Underneath,* beautiful films that nevertheless often feel weighted down by Soderbergh's intense concentration on form. The energy and playfulness of *Out of Sight,* on the other hand, with its jump cuts, freeze frames, saturated colors and gritty textures, is reminiscent of *Schizopolis'* freewheeling looseness.

"It seems odd that one would inform the other, especially since they're so different, but it's really true," says Soderbergh. "[*Schizopolis*] woke me up." While he wasn't worried about maintaining that newfound energy, Soderbergh was concerned about finding a film that would give him the kind of big budget that would allow him to exploit that energy even further. *Out of Sight* "was an opportunity to put into use some things I had learned in other movies, from *The Underneath* to *Schizopolis* and *Gray's Anatomy,* which were real great testing grounds for me. I was fortunate that Casey Silver [chairman of Universal Pictures], who I've made two unsuccessful movies for, continued to think of me for projects like this."

It was Silver who brought Scott Frank's script to Soderbergh's attention. The director knew it was something he could handle as soon as he finished reading it: "It was character-driven, performance-reliant, it played to things I feel comfortable with." He also felt ready, again, to tackle a large production. But conventional Hollywood wisdom says that you don't just hand over a $49 million star vehicle like *Out of Sight* to someone with an art-house reputation and a commensurate track record at the box office. In spite of Silver's support, Soderbergh says, he had his job cut out for him convincing Jersey Films that he was their man. "I had to go chase this, I had to audition for it," he says. "I had to talk to Jersey Films, I had to talk to Clooney. There were a lot of people they were talking to, and I was probably the coldest one on the list. I had to go in and say I really feel like I know how to do this."

As producer Michael Shamberg of Jersey Films tells it, Soderbergh was always on the short list ("we're fans of his work"), and his references to Hal Ashby's *The Last Detail* and William Friedkin's *The French Connection* put him over the top at their first meeting. Clooney, in particular, was jazzed on Soderbergh. If anything, Shamberg says, the director was "overly defensive" during the process, even to the point of refusing to screen *Schizopolis* for him. "Later, he gave me a video, and I thought it was great," says Shamberg. "I asked him why he didn't want to show it, and he said he thought we wouldn't want to hire him if we saw it." Apart from promising Silver that he was "not going to make a $49 million version of *The Underneath*," Soderbergh pretty much had free rein to make the film he wanted. The only pressure that he felt, he says, came from within. "I wanted it to be good because potentially more people would see it than any other film I'd made, and you don't want to blow that."

So what happens if *Out of Sight* doesn't perform at the box office? (The film earned about $12.9 million on its opening weekend.) As the most obvious outsider, Soderbergh is an easy would-be scapegoat, which for a lot of reasons makes this one of the riskiest films of his career. If he ends up alienating both his core indie supporters and Hollywood, he may be relegated to self-financed stylistic freak-outs indefinitely. Soderbergh himself isn't too concerned. He's got projects lined up—in addition to *A Confederacy of Dunces,* there's something small he hopes to start by the end of the year and possibly another film with Clooney, a comedy about the early years of foot-ball. As for *Out of Sight*, he isn't making any predictions, but his experience in making it has put him in something of an optimistic mood. "Let's put it this way," he says. "It doesn't seem greedy to make a movie once every nine years that people show up to go see. If I'm the cinematic equivalent of the locust, it seems like I'm coming up on that time. And if so, that's great, because then I'll be able to coast for another eight years and make some more interesting movies."

The Flashback Kid

SHEILA JOHNSTON/1999

WHEN *SEX, LIES, AND VIDEOTAPE* won the Palme d'or in Cannes ten years ago, before making more than $100 million worldwide (on a budget of $1.2 million), Steven Soderbergh, then 26, became overnight the poster child of independent American cinema. The blockbuster event movies pioneered by George Lucas and Steven Spielberg in the mid '70s had dominated international markets for over a decade; Soderbergh's brilliant debut pointed to a different way forward. But then his next movies bombed: the angst-ridden *Kafka* (1991); *King of the Hill* (1993), the story of a small boy struggling to survive the Depression; the glacial *film noir The Underneath* (1995). Interviewed about the last, Soderbergh launched into a long, morose attack: "I've lost interest in the cinematic baggage you have to use to make a film palatable for a mass audience."

Unsurprisingly, his career went quiet. He took on a string of behind-the-scenes producing and script-writing assignments including *Pleasantville* and the ill-fated U.S. remake of *Night Watch*. Plans for *Quiz Show* foundered when Robert Redford hijacked the project. Soderbergh the director appeared to be all washed up: a one-hit wonder.

In fact he had gone to ground to make *Schizopolis*, a no-budget, Dadaesque comedy in which Soderbergh himself plays the tragic-comic hero struggling with his sense of alienation and his failing marriage (his wife was played by the director's own soon-to-be ex-spouse Betsy Brantley). The film's reception at its Cannes premiere in 1996 was rather more muted than the ovation that

From *Sight and Sound*, November 1999. Reprinted by permission.

had greeted *sex,lies,* with a torrent of bored and bewildered audience members diving for the exit. With his next film, *Gray's Anatomy* (1996), a small-scale piece made with the monologuist Spalding Gray, Soderbergh seemed to have disappeared for good beneath the radar.

But then in 1998 he bounced back triumphantly with an unpromising-sounding assignment as director-for-hire on an adaptation of Elmore Leonard's novel *Out of Sight,* about a failed bank robber and a deputy federal marshall who can't decide whether to arrest the charming felon or fall in love with him. Sexy, elegant and profoundly romantic (a new departure for a director whose work has often been regarded as somewhat cerebral), it was hailed by critics as his best film since *sex, lies.* His return to favour continues with *The Limey,* which played out of competition at Cannes this year. The story of an English ex-convict (Terence Stamp) who travels to Los Angeles to investigate his daughter's death following her involvement with a hedonistic record producer (Peter Fonda), it is on one level a straight revenge thriller with strong echoes of *Get Carter,* while its spaced-out feel and bravura kaleidoscopic editing make it play like a homage to the formal experimentation of '60s and '70s cinema.

Soderbergh has been described by one U.S. interviewer, a little patronisingly if not altogether inaccurately, as a "goofy, balding, loveable geek." But underneath that persona, thinly concealed, are a steely intelligence and formidable self-awareness. And though he has worked within an astonishing range of registers—from the avant-garde *Schizopolis,* through the quintessential U.S. indie sensibility of *sex, lies* and the arty, black-and-white, middle-European universe of *Kafka,* to such demi-Hollywood genre pieces as *Out of Sight* and *The Limey*—he insists adamantly on the continuity of his work.

SHEILA JOHNSTON: *You use a very complex chronological structure in* The Limey—*was that written into the script or created at the editing stage?*
STEVEN SODERBERGH: I shot it that way. My whole line while we were making it was, "If we do our job right this is *Get Carter* as made by Alain Resnais," which I know spells big box office! I was trying to get a sense of how your mind sifts through things and I felt I could get away with a certain amount of abstraction because the backbone of the movie is so straight. Even so, my first version was so layered and deconstructed even people who had worked on the movie didn't understand it. So I had to start working back to find a balance, which I did through screenings for friends: writers, actors,

producers, directors, a new group of guinea pigs each time. At one point
Artisan [the production company] wanted a public preview. But I said, "For
a movie like this it's worthless: it's going to score terribly and I'll get nothing
I haven't already got by inviting intelligent, creative people to give me
ideas." A week before we were going to do it, they called and said, "You're
right, it's a waste of money. Just finish it the way you're going to finish it and
we'll figure out the rest."

S J : *The film's steeped in the mood of the '6os, though you're a little young to have
had much direct experience of that counterculture.*
S S : I've been working for some time on a book of interviews with Richard
Lester called *Getting Away with It* and I asked him a lot about that period.
Mostly we talked about the gradual shift from optimism to disillusion. I was
whining about something and then I added, "Still, has there ever been a
generation that hasn't said, 'It's never been this bad'?" He said, "Yeah, in the
'6os." But as soon as it became apparent that the youth movement was an
ongoing economic force, it began to be co-opted into mainstream culture,
and that—combined with other things like harder drugs becoming available—was when things started to shift. When Lester made two trips to San
Francisco to research and shoot *Petulia* in 1966 and 1967 he said he could feel
a very strong, dark undercurrent on the second visit that wasn't there on the
first. That's the feeling that permeates *The Limey.* There's one guy whose
dreams of himself were lost in prison and another whose dreams were probably never even his own: he just took everybody else's and made money out
of them.

S J : *How important was it to cast two icons of '6os cinema?*
S S : Both Terence Stamp and Peter Fonda have baggage that's not only specific to the '6os but has to do with a refusal to compromise: they've stayed
pretty true to themselves all these years. But I wasn't trying to turn in a pastiche—though clearly when we had Peter Fonda driving in a fast vehicle up
the coast, I thought, "We've gotta get Steppenwolf." Terence seemed like a
Who kind of guy—in fact his brother, Chris Stamp, was one of the people
who discovered them.

S J : *One of the film's most remarkable features is your use of scenes from Ken
Loach's 1967 movie* Poor Cow, *in which Stamp played another thief, to show his
character in flashbacks.*

s s : In cinema you can follow actors over a long period—you can really see the accumulation of someone's life experience. So the idea of using Ken's film was intriguing, and as far as I know no one had done that before. There was a lengthy process to get the rights because *Poor Cow* was based on a book by Nell Dunn, and Carol White, who was in the scenes we wanted to use, was dead. It went on for months and didn't get completely resolved until we were editing. Then I met with Ken and said, "Look, I've got this cleared up legally, but morally I can't do it if you think it's offensive." But when I explained what I was doing, he said it was fine.

s j : *When you took receipt of your Palme d'or for* sex, lies, and videotape *you said: "It's all downhill from here." Do you now feel that has been true of your career?*
s s : I was being facetious, but what I meant was that it seemed unlikely I would ever again be the recipient of such unified acclaim. A lot of people never are, and to get it for my first movie seemed almost comical. The Palme d'or helped me hugely—it made a name for me in Europe, where people sometimes like my movies more than they do in the States—but if *sex, lies* had made only half a million dollars nobody would be talking about it today. It was modest piece with modest aspirations that happened to be what people wanted to see in a way I obviously haven't been able to duplicate. It was pure chance: I have a strong feeling that had it been made a year later it wouldn't have hit in the same way.

s j : *Unlike many younger American independent filmmakers, you didn't use the success of your first film as a springboard to a commercial Hollywood career. Are you happy now with the choices you made?*
s s : Let's put it this way, I don't regret any of them. There have been good ones and bad ones, but I look back and think, "That's an eclectic group of movies that, for better or worse, belong to me." I turned down a lot of studio stuff—or rather traditional studio stuff, because two of my films were made by Universal—until *Out of Sight,* which seemed the perfect blend of what I do and the resources a studio can provide.

s j : *What is the difference between coming in on a preexisting project and creating a film from scratch?*

s s : With a screenplay that didn't come from you, you get on that train and it takes a while to start driving it. But you work your way through each car until you get to the front, and once you're close to shooting there's really no difference. By then you usually have a healthy disrespect for—or sense of detachment from—the material, even if you've written it yourself. When we rehearsed *Out of Sight* I started cutting lines because, though Elmore Leonard writes great dialogue, it seemed in scenes like the last one there wasn't a lot to be said. That's one of the differences between a book and a movie. I met someone recently who was in *Days of Heaven* and she said there was lots of dialogue in the script, but when they got on the set Terence Malick would go, "Don't say anything." When you look at the film you realise that he ended up having to write all that voiceover in post-production because nobody said anything so nobody knew what was going on! You think, "Oh, that's such a great example of stripping everything away," and then you find out why he did it. Sometimes it's better not to know too much.

s j : *Along with Barry Sonnenfeld's* Get Shorty *and Quentin Tarantino's* Jackie Brown, Out of Sight *ushered in a revival of interest in Elmore Leonard, whose work had rarely been successfully translated into film.*
s s : Quentin Tarantino's rise has so much to do with Elmore Leonard's world, as he would be the first to admit, that by the time a 'real' Leonard adaptation showed up in the form of *Get Shorty,* everyone had been prepared by *Reservoir Dogs* and *Pulp Fiction* for that tone. Actually *Get Shorty, Jackie Brown* and *Out of Sight* are textbook examples of what a director does, because they all three feel like Elmore Leonard movies but are completely different from each other. When you try to explain what it is you do, this is it: you take a piece of material, it's filtered through your eyes and ears, and it comes out with a very specific atmosphere.

s j : *Your films have a lyrical, dreamlike quality that gives them an almost European flavour.*
s s : When I was at university I'd see one, sometimes two movies a night: films like *8½* or *The Third Man* or *A Hard Day's Night.* I was drawn to European cinema—its approach to character was more complicated and stylistically it seemed more rigorous and interesting. When you see an Antonioni film at an impressionable age it has a huge impact. Everything on screen is there for

a reason—even *Zabriskie Point,* which is odd and flawed, is astonishing to look at.

S J : *What's your prognosis for the new generation of U.S. indie directors?*

S S : It's much harder for them today. The expectations are much higher and the competition is much fiercer. It's easier to get a film made now because *sex, lies* and a handful of others have made money. But it's much more difficult to get it released because the marketplace is very competitive and distributors are not as adventurous as they used to be.

S J : *What about your future plans?*

S S : I've just made *Erin Brockovich,* which is an aggressively linear reality-based drama about a twice-divorced mother-of-three living at a very low income level who talks herself into a job answering the phone and ends up putting together a case against a large California utility company that results in the biggest direct-action lawsuit settlement in history. She's played by Julia Roberts—if you're trying to sneak something under the wire, by which I mean an adult, intelligent film with no sequel potential, no merchandising, no high concept and no big hook, it's nice to have one of the world's most bankable stars sneaking under with you. Other than that, I'm riding off madly in all directions. I've always had one foot in and one foot out of Hollywood—that's what makes me comfortable. Together with Scott Frank, who adapted *Out of Sight,* I'm writing an original spec screenplay that's a multi-character murder mystery along the lines of an Agatha Christie. And I'm making notes for *Son of Schizopolis*—the sequel to the film nobody saw.

Straight Man: Joking Around, or Not, with *Limey* Director Steven Soderbergh

SCOTT KELTON JONES/1999

TOWARD THE END OF HIS PUBLISHED JOURNAL on the making of the watershed indie film *sex, lies, and videotape*—his 1989 million-dollar feature debut that jump-started the independent-film-is-hip craze, put the Sundance Film Festival on the map, upset Spike Lee's *Do the Right Thing* for the top award at Cannes, and went on to capture the American psyche and almost 25 million dollars during its theatrical run—director Steven Soderbergh worries more than once that he's coming across as too serious in his interviews. In this one, occurring some 10 years later—during which time Soderbergh has made a handful of entertaining films with plenty of deadpan funny moments—it doesn't seem an issue, at least while it's going on. This conversation, much like Soderbergh's films, jumps around, but it's full of interesting, insightful, and funny revelations about everything from French New Wave cinema to how irked he was when *Rocky* won the Best Picture Academy Award over *All the President's Men* ("I knew right then it was all over"). But once the whole thing is transcribed onto a printed page, he just comes across so . . . serious.

It's because Soderbergh, like many of his films, can't really be taken straight-on. You need to know the context and the character. He seems simple and straightforward, but he surprises with unexpected flair and wry, almost sublime wit, as though he's thoroughly tickling himself and hasn't bothered to make sure everyone else is in tune. George Clooney, Soderbergh's leading man in last year's underseen but sparkling cops-and-robbers-

From *Dallas Observer*, October 14, 1999. Reprinted by permission.

in-love caper flick *Out of Sight,* has said of him, "Seven has a dry sense of humor. He's evil is what he is. And often as you can do a movie with guys like that, do it."

Clooney's next chance may be with *Leatherheads,* a romantic comedy set against beginnings of professional football that was green-lighted back when *Out of Sight* had blockbuster buzz—meaning, just before it just plain busted. The project isn't on Soderbergh's short list, but he says the two men "keep hatching these plans—we're still circling it," as though he and Clooney are vultures trying to make the most of their carrion.

"We both need more . . . *momentum,* more than we had behind us on the heels of *Out of Sight,*" he says. "Its commercial performance didn't give us the last nudge we needed to push it through. But we just talked about this the other week. He's got *Three Kings,* and he just finished the Coen Brothers movie [*O Brother, Where Are Thou?*], which will be in Cannes next year and by all accounts is going to be hilarious. And now I've got . . ." Long pause. ". . . *The Limey,* which will probably solidify my standing as a cult failure." During his halt, you can almost see him smile through the phone, though the tone seems to dip toward melancholy.

Soderbergh is referring to his new film *The Limey,* which feels so akin to *Out of Sight,* it's almost like a low-budget, indie-spirited do-over. Both films revitalize crime genre motifs by using stylistic flourishes, narrative gymnastics, and memorable characters that can be as likeable, as endearing, as they are hard-boiled. And, maybe, it's a reminder that the roots of both these works can be traced back to Soderbergh's underappreciated, low-budget shot-in-Austin indie film, *The Underneath,* a 1995 stylistic neo-noir that disappointed only those who went into it expecting something approximating Burt Lancaster's teeth-gnashing in the original.

"I've made three crime films, but it's not a genre I really feel any affinity for," Soderbergh says. If he's aware of the irony that some critics might say the same thing, he's not letting on. "I guess it's an easy genre to inject with your own preoccupations. Usually, you have a spine that's pretty solid, pretty easy for people to grasp. The conflicts are really clear, and that gives you freedom to sort of mess around a little bit."

And mess around he does in *The Limey.* Once again, he uses flashbacks, flashforwards, and flash*way*backs, cutting back and forth between scenes that appear to be taking place at the same time. It was an effect he used in *Out of Sight, The Underneath,* and, to a much lesser but still crucial effect, in *sex, lies, and videotape.* It's as though he's skipping around the time line, turning yesterdays into tomorrows and tomorrows into right now. Soderbergh also mixes film stock and, in *The Limey's* most flashy gimmick (at least in a really film-geeky way), uses footage of star Terence Stamp culled from a minor role he played in Ken Loach's 1967 film *Poor Cow.* The result is a film that is essentially a straightforward boiler-room plot you've seen a million times—an ex-con hunts down the bad guys who killed his daughter—turned inside out and upside down, giving the characters a resonance and the story some themes that transcend the genre. "Simple revenge film with a lot of '60s baggage" is Soderbergh's dismissive tag line for his film. "When I was finishing *Out of Sight,* there were some ideas about how to play with narrative that had occurred to me that weren't really appropriate for it. Cinema allows you to play around and push narrative so well and so easily, maybe better than any other art form. And I thought, gee, I really want to try some of this other stuff." So Soderbergh called Lem Dobbs (*Dark City*), a screenwriter he had collaborated with in 1991 on the ambitious if not completely on-target literary psychological thriller *Kafka,* to revisit *The Limey.* It was an idea they had discussed seven years ago and had even thought about doing after Soderbergh's 1993 solid but occasionally doddering coming-of-age drama *King of the Hill.* If nothing else, the two men knew they wanted Terence Stamp, who played the title role in 1962's *Billy Budd,* and *Easy Rider's* Peter Fonda in the roles of bad guy and worse guy.

"We both liked the idea of an older guy in the lead, for obvious commercial reasons. Those films are so popular," Soderbergh says, almost letting slip a chuckle. "And we were both interested in the '60s and the dream of the '60s that sort of died out for a lot of reasons, and sort of the doppelgänger of putting in guys who have always gone their own way, have been in and out of favor over the course of their careers, and have recently come back into people's minds. Besides, it's Captain America vs. Billy Budd—that's kind of a cool idea."

Using the *Poor Cow* footage was also just another cool idea, Soderbergh says, not a deliberate attempt at a sequel. "I told Lem, wouldn't it be great, since Terence was a movie star in the '60s, wouldn't it be great if we could find some footage or something and stick it in the movie. And Lem sent me a fax the next morning that said, 'Well, it should be *Poor Cow.* [Stamp] plays this young thief who gets busted and goes to prison.' The character's name happened to be Dave Wilson, and we were looking for a last name—we figured you'd never really know his first name—a terse, kind of generic-sounding last name. Coincidentally, we thought Wilson sounded good. So, it's an accidental sequel of sorts. It's almost a variation on the *Rosencrantz and Guildenstern Are Dead* thing. We take someone who is a minor character and see where he is 30 years later. But it's not exactly the same character. Our Wilson has a daughter. They have a little boy in the other film. So, really there's a lot of stuff I wanted to take, but I just couldn't get that boy out of there."

Soderbergh almost wasn't able to swipe any of *Poor Cow* for use in *The Limey*. Although he started negotiating for the rights before his film even started shooting, the filmmakers didn't secure them until after *The Limey* was in the can. "There were times where it looked like it just wasn't going to happen," Soderbergh says. "Talk about a terrifying way to shoot. I literally felt that the movie just wouldn't work without it."

But surely he had a contingency plan?

"No, no. It was really all or nothing. It took a couple of well-placed phone calls from friends in the right spots . . ." He pauses, as though talking about it suddenly makes him realize how dangerous his high-wire act really was. "Ah, yes, it was a scary shoot."

However, his next film, due out in the spring, wasn't a scary shoot at all. This, despite the fact that it's *Erin Brockovich,* which stars Julia Roberts as a young lawyer chasing cancer-causing companies.

"I really loved the material," Soderbergh says. "And I actually thought it could be absolutely perfect for her, that she could be really great in it. We were both hooking up at a good time. I was ready to make this kind of movie, which is unlike anything I've made before. She was ready to make it, and it was unlike anything she'd ever really done before. I think it's a real strong piece of work"

Soderbergh also has *Traffik* on the horizon. "It's about drugs," he says glibly, not offering much more information than that it's based on a British miniseries from 1989—coincidentally, the same year he first broke into the spotlight and helped revolutionize the indie film market. Hard to believe it was just 10 years ago since the release of *sex, lies, and videotape;* hard to believe "Sundance" has been a verb for only a decade. Soderbergh, actually, is thankful to have been there at the beginning of the art-house-as-commerce revolution—if only because it was better to have been there first, rather than second or last.

"I feel very lucky," he says, when asked how it felt to have been the man who created the indie-film feeding frenzy, who helped turn Miramax into a household name outside Harvey Weinstein's house. After all, he says, better to create the frenzy than be devoured by it. "Now there's too much attention, too many expectations, too much coverage for people who haven't done anything yet. I wouldn't want to be coming up now. Too many interviews." That's a joke, right?

Emotion, Truth, and Celluloid

MICHAEL SRAGOW/2000

IN 1995, STEVEN SODERBERGH had reached a career dead end, just six years after igniting the independent-film craze with his debut film, *sex, lies, and videotape*—a movie he recently (and correctly) characterized for the British film mag *Sight and Sound* as "a modest piece with modest aspirations that happened to be what people wanted to see in a way I obviously haven't been able to duplicate." His pastiche *Kafka* (1991) and Depression-childhood saga *King of the Hill* (1993) didn't spark with audiences or generate critical or cult followings. He simply floundered in his flop '95 neonoir *The Underneath*, smothering snappy lines and arresting arcs of character with arty coups de cinema.

But in 1998, he came up with *Out of Sight*, a smart, engaging action comedy about the love that ignites between a bank robber (George Clooney) and a deputy federal marshal (Jennifer Lopez) when she stumbles into his jailbreak and gets to know him in the trunk of a getaway car. It won best picture of the year from the National Society of Film Critics, beating out favorites like *Shakespeare in Love* and *Saving Private Ryan*. (The group also named Soderbergh, not Spielberg, best director.)

And Soderbergh's *The Limey*, which opened last fall and ranks high on many a 10-best list, is an unexpectedly touching act of hard-boiled cinematic seduction. It tells the story of a canny British ex-con (Terence Stamp) who flies to L.A. to exact revenge on the man who killed his daughter. Soderbergh

This article (January 6, 2000) first appeared in Salon.com, http://www.Salon.com. An online version remains in the Salon archives. Reprinted with permission.

puts this basic thriller setup into a time-hopping form that resembles an elaborate paper cutout—the kind that comes all raveled up and reveals its true meaning when the last piece is uncovered.

Like *Out of Sight, The Limey* is a light movie, not a superficial one. Soderbergh has learned that an audience will follow any director to what lies underneath as long as he keeps his film expressive on the surface. History and current events meld in the ex-con's brain, as he thinks back on his daughter and her mother. But Soderbergh does more than play memory games with fleet flash-forwards and flashbacks. At the end we realize that the entire film has been the gangster remembering things past and judging his own culpability.

The Limey is a salute to 1967 filmmaking: It echoes John Boorman's *Point Blank* and actually uses footage of Stamp playing a young thief in Kenneth Loach's *Poor Cow.* So it's wonderfully appropriate that Soderbergh has come forth with a book on filmmaker Richard Lester, who by 1967 had already made *A Hard Day's Night, Help!* and the audacious *How I Won the War.*

Soderbergh's *Getting Away with It, Or: The Further Adventures of the Luckiest Bastard You Ever Saw—also Starring Richard Lester as the Man Who Knew More Than He Was Asked* was published in Great Britain in 1999. It treats movie fans to a funny, prismatically illuminating experience.

In addition to his penetrating interviews with Lester, Soderbergh sandwiches in the candid journal of a chaotic year in his own career—1996, right after *The Underneath* and right before he landed the directing job on *Out of Sight.* He was finishing up two idiosyncratic, small films, *Schizopolis* and *Gray's Anatomy,* while doing script work for hire, staging Jonathan Reynolds' play *Geniuses,* helping to produce *Pleasantville* and struggling to mount an adaptation of *A Confederacy of Dunces.*

What's neat about *Getting Away with It* is that you witness Soderbergh renewing himself as he talks to Lester. The younger director opens up to the older one, who delves into matters as different as evolutionary theory and military milestones. Even the structure of the book expresses Soderbergh's burgeoning energy: It's a delicious parody of the exhaustive, multi-part director interview—a specialty of Soderbergh's own publisher, Faber and Faber. Soderbergh's readers were the first in their arthouse or multiplex to hear the name of *Being John Malkovich* screenwriter Charlie Kaufman. In 1996 Soderbergh had tried to launch another Kaufman script, *Human Nature.* The director's readers were also the first to learn of "tortious interference," the legal concept at the center of Michael Mann's *The Insider:* Paramount invoked it to prevent Soderbergh and his *Limey* producer Scott Kramer from setting up *A Confederacy of Dunces* as a co-venture with other companies. Most important, the book delivers a privileged glimpse into the sensibilities of filmmakers who use sophisticated film syntax to heighten emotion and find novel ways of embodying old storytelling values of romance, suspense and catharsis. When I phoned Soderbergh in L.A. in December, he was taking a pause from his forthcoming feature *Erin Brockovich* (due out in March). He instantly made clear that Lester isn't his only idol. He said that *Erin Brockovich,* a socially conscious character study starring Julia Roberts, fit "the John Huston plan for career longevity: Never become too hip or faddish."

MICHAEL SRAGOW: *When will* Getting Away with It *get an official U.S. publication?*
STEVEN SODERBERGH: Most of Faber and Faber's stuff usually shows up here, but as you probably gleaned from the book they can be somewhat erratic. I still haven't got my box of author's copies!

MS: *That's unfortunate, because it has a lot of topical hooks, including the first mention between book covers of screenwriter Charlie Kaufman. Your comment on his* Human Nature *script—you call it indescribable except for being "very weird" and "hysterically funny"—hits home for anyone who's seen* Being John Malkovich.
SS: About four years ago, I asked a friend of mine who had some experience in the development-reading world to help me find something to do. She called two weeks after I said I'd hire her and told me "I found the guy." She sent me *Malkovich* and *Human Nature.* At that time *Malkovich* was already set up; it was obvious that this guy was going to happen. I got to hang out with him while we were trying to get *Human Nature* set up, and I liked him enormously.

MS: *I really enjoyed interviewing him, but he didn't want to reveal too much of himself or analyze his own work.*
SS: He's probably, in the long run, pretty smart to do that. I still have fantasies myself of pulling a Terrence Malick. It's really a silly problem, but it's frustrating to be in a situation where you become bored with speaking about what you love to do for a living. You find yourself hating not just the sound

of your voice, but hearing it make the work that you do sound boring. It's a terrible sensation. You definitely get to a point where you feel like a homeless person babbling on a corner, saying the same thing over and over to very little effect.

In the long run I don't know how much good talking does. I don't think audiences pay too much attention—people who want to go to a movie will go. When you look at the selling part of the business, everything that everybody does for every movie feels the same. We did a ton of press for *The Limey*. Maybe it would have done even worse if we hadn't, but I can't say what helped and what didn't.

M S : *The Limey is loved by the people I know who've seen it; I'm surprised to hear you say it didn't do well.*
S S : It did really well in New York and L.A., so for a lot of people the perception of it is that it did fine.

M S : *Much of your book is about trying to maintain enthusiasm and energy over the course of a career. There's a wonderful interplay between you and Lester— almost as if you started the book out of devotion to his movies but then had these revelations about your own films.*
S S : It emerged from this period when I felt I had to start over again. I think there are two components to doing that successfully. One is regaining enthusiasm about your own work. The other is regaining enthusiasm about other people's work.

When I see people who I think have become either cynical artistically or just competitive to the point of self-destruction, what they share is the loss of appreciation for anything that anybody else is doing. Seeing something good should make you want to do something good; if you're not careful, you can lose that. And that can hurt you. I still get a charge out of seeing a really good movie or reading a really good book or watching *The Sopranos* on TV.

Working my way through Lester's films, and doing these interviews with him, I was reinvigorating myself. And there was also something cautionary about it. Lester did stop working for a variety of reasons. So for me there is the element, whether it's spoken or not, of "Wow, will that happen to me? And to all of us?"

M S : *There are recurring topics and themes in the book. You talk a lot about one of*

Lester's favorite actors, Roy Kinnear, who died after he fell from a horse during the making of Lester's last film, The Return of the Musketeers. *You touch on whether Lester's atheism made him feel more responsible for the accident than he would have if he'd believed in a divine plan, and hastened his departure from filmmaking. It makes the reader confront the moviemaker as a person, not a technician.*

SS: I think that's what we were both hoping for. Between the Q and A and the journal, I just thought it was perhaps relevant to somebody to portray the process of what it's like to be a person who happens to do this for a living as opposed to a portrait of a filmmaker. It was hard. I was working while I was doing it and it was a massive editing job. I had 35 hours of interviews with him, and the journal I had was probably five times the length of what you read.

MS: *And then you have all these self-deprecating footnotes, which touch on comic battles with your editors at Faber and Faber. You have a jokey "Note From Your Publisher" and two mock author's notes, including an introduction that will contain an "Awesome display of ego disguised as humility; joke about same." Even the title and the cover design make your book feel as irreverent as a Lester movie.*

SS: The footnote idea came late because I felt something was missing; one more deconstructed element was needed. So in the last two weeks just before I turned it in, I came up with the idea of a fictional person at Faber who hates me. The copy editors at Faber got a huge kick out of the "inside" view of how the company works.

I mean, I love all the director books they do, "So-and-so on so-and-so"; I've got all of them. But I thought, We've got to tart this up a bit. We've got to put on some bells and whistles, so if somebody picks it up off the shelf they'll feel they have to buy it.

MS: *A lot of younger directors, as different as Danny Boyle (*Trainspotting*) and Stacy Cochran (*My New Gun*) and Michael Patrick Jann (*Drop Dead Gorgeous*), have taken inspiration from Lester's movies.*

SS: And I know in some cases they are taking the right things from his work—not just the visual dexterity of, Oh, if I shoot a lot of images and do a lot of cutting, it will be just like a Richard Lester movie. There's a lot more thought behind it than that. We would all do well to look behind the surface at some of the ideas he's trying to put across, because he's an intelligent guy and he expressed a point of view—especially, in his peak years, about society at large.

I think he has a genuine interest and appreciation for people who do not have power. And I think that's getting lost a lot these days. I was talking to a buddy of mine who went into a meeting with some executives and they were describing a lead character in a project they wanted to do. "He's one of these guys, he really has the town wired; he knows everyone and he's doing all these things." We were just sitting there going, "Who is that? We don't know anybody like that. And who, of the people who would go see this movie, knows anyone like that?" The idea that you can make a movie about an ordinary person is almost gone.

MS: *Usually, when you talk about a director of ideas, you think of someone cerebral or self-conscious. But Lester at his best is downright blithe about getting his ideas to the screen.*

SS: That's the other thing that I took from him, which has helped me enormously in the last few films, including the one I'm finishing now (*Erin Brockovich*). How should I describe it? Tossing things off, instead of being labored about what you do. I'm serious about what I do, but I think there's a real benefit to not being precious and working quickly and going strictly on instinct. It's something I lost and I absolutely got back from him.

MS: *Because* Out of Sight *and* The Limey *have such stylistic confidence, it's odd to think of them as in any way "tossed-off." What you call relying on instinct must also mean relying on whatever craftsmanlike reflexes you've built up.*

SS: I had the luxury of making a first film that was successful enough to afford me a lot of mistakes. The good news was I took advantage of them. By the time *Out of Sight* rolled around I felt pretty light on my feet and secure in my ability to work in a way that was expedient but detailed. That was my seventh film—if I was paying attention at all I should have been able to do that!

But as we both know, a lot of people aren't paying attention. Directing has become the best entry-level job in show business. You have to keep your eye on the long term—which is why I understand what Charlie Kaufman is doing. I try to be careful about things I do and not promote myself separately apart from a film I'm talking about. I've never taken a possessory credit, because anything that furthers the idea of you as a brand name is risky—because people get tired of certain brands.

M S : *Lester is frank about decisions he made that have sometimes been called forced and inorganic. For example, he admits that he conceived the elaborate structure of* Petulia *because he was afraid that if he didn't, it might have come off as "a romantic novelette."*

S S : In point of fact, does it matter that Lester and the writers who worked on *Petulia* sort of deconstructed it because otherwise it would be a terrible melodrama? No. The bottom line is, that's a great film, no matter how you cut it. Everything is working against it being a terrible melodrama, from the way it's cast to the way the performances are pitched on the set to the way it's composed and cut. That's why it works—it's because he's cutting against the grain of what's inherent in that material. Sometimes that's a mistake, but in that case it certainly isn't.

Talking with Richard Lester reminded me of how rigorous you have to be; conceptually, you have to sit down and make sure you're wringing everything out of the material that you should be wringing out of it. What frustrated me about *The Underneath* was that I felt I wasn't rigorous with it. On the one hand, maybe there should be an international cultural police force—so when someone like me says, "I want to splice an armored-car heist movie together with Antonioni's *Red Desert,*" they come and stop you. But on the other hand, if you make a revisionist nonlinear noir movie, there are more places to go with it than I did in *The Underneath.* I was not at a time in my career when I understood that; and I was just feeling sort of dry.

M S : *Out of Sight* is juicy—*just as ambitious stylistically, but with emotional coherence and impact. When I first saw the opening flourish of George Clooney ripping off his tie and the jacket of his suit, I was happy to accept it as an expression of anger and frustration, without knowing whether it would fit into the rest of the movie.*

S S : Absolutely. But I don't think you can be arbitrary about that stuff. In *Out of Sight* I knew I was going to use freeze frames and zooms and jump-cutting, but I was also trying to be very aware of the reason for each of them. For instance, intercutting Clooney and Jennifer Lopez in the cocktail lounge and the hotel room: The reason I was doing that was because I wanted to make the sense of intimacy and electricity more palpable to the audience. I thought back to that sequence in *Don't Look Now,* and how those two scenes

of Donald Sutherland and Julie Christie making love and getting dressed suggested an intimacy that was stronger than either of those scenes alone.

As for *The Limey:* That is about a guy who cannot stay rooted in the present. He is completely dislocated.

M S :   *From the start, the cutting in* The Limey *conveys the play of thought and
memory, but I wasn't prepared for the cumulative effect. The whole movie hinges
on a speech and a gesture that the daughter of the antihero (Terence Stamp) makes
to him as a little girl and to the villain (Peter Fonda) as a woman. Via flashbacks,
a woman who is dead carries the film's emotional weight—and turns it from
revenge film to tragedy.*

S S :   I remember the day when the screenwriter, Lem Dobbs, and I were at
his house, talking about the climactic sequence and my belief that there
needed to be an emotional reason for why all of this happened. We came up
with the idea that when finally forced to tell his side of the story, Peter Fonda's character would essentially repeat something that had happened to Terence Stamp's character. And the result is not explosion but implosion.

Looking back at the movies we were riffing on, *Point Blank* and *Get Carter,*
I realized that I love those movies but they're not the most emotional experiences in the world. They're very compelling and they're pretty cold. And I
thought that if we were going to do one of those movies, we needed to have
a strong emotional undercurrent. When you see most shoot'em-up revenge
movies you don't get too emotionally invested. The combination of how we
thought about it and casting Terence and finding that footage from *Poor Cow*
helped build the quiet emotional foundation that pays off in the end.

M S :   *When Lester was in his prime, he would get an idea and get a writer and just
go off and do it. Are you able to operate the same way? Would you want to?*

S S :   I don't have a lot of stuff that I'm contemplating or attached to or developing; I try not to work more than one or two movies ahead of myself. I tend
to feel differently about things when I get out the other end of a movie. For
instance, there's *Erin Brockovich,* which I'm finishing now. Jersey Films had
spoken to me about it right after I did *Out of Sight* for them, and it just
sounded terrible to me. But when I got out the other end of *The Limey,* it
sounded like the perfect thing to do; it was so different from my previous
two films, and so unlike anything I had made before.

MS: *All I know is that it's based on a real-life story about a woman (Julia Roberts)*
involved in researching a health-related lawsuit against a utility company. It
sounds like A Civil Action.

SS: But it's not about the lawsuit, it's about her, and that's what drew me
to it. There's one courtroom scene halfway through the film that's two minutes long. I just found her character fascinating. And the story was so aggressively linear that it required a completely different set of disciplines than *The*
Limey or *Out of Sight.* I had to be a different filmmaker to do what I thought
was appropriate for telling it. There are movies where you can get away with
a certain amount of standing between the screen and the audience and waving your hands. This isn't one of them. You need an understanding of when
you need to let things play and not be intrusive. At the same time, I hope
you'll absolutely recognize *Erin Brockovich* as something that I've done,
because there is an aesthetic at play that relates it to films I've made before.
And it does have a protagonist who is at odds with the surroundings; I tend
to be drawn to those. Here it happens to be a lower-income woman. It was
fun to make a movie where the protagonist was female and was in every
scene of the film.

   If you're a certain kind of filmmaker, everything is personal, whether a
movie is about yourself or not. But I think, for the most part, people who
write about film have a very limited idea of what personal expression is and
how it can manifest itself. As a result you often find directors being encouraged to make "personal films" when they would probably grow faster and go
further if they began to look outside of themselves. That was the real turning
point for me: I wasn't interested in making films about me anymore, and my
take on things. I thought, "I've got to get out of the house!" And I've had
more fun and I think the work is better since that occurred to me. I'm interested in other people's experiences—filtered through mine, obviously. I'm
absolutely as connected to *Erin Brockovich* emotionally as I was to *sex, lies.*
Some people just either can't believe that, or don't want to believe it, or just
don't understand the process. You don't spend a year and a half on something you don't give a shit about.

MS: *There's a great passage in the book where you ponder an American director's*
alternatives: ". . . make stupid Hollywood movies? Or fake highbrow movies with
people who would be as cynical about hiring me to make a 'smart' movie as others
are when they hire the latest hot action director to make some blastfest?"

ss: What was bugging me was that both those possibilities were equally calculating, which I think is the enemy of good work. Now what I have managed, luckily, because *Out of Sight* was waved in front of me and I jumped at it, is to find a certain meeting place. As somebody once put to me, bluntly, "If you think Hollywood movies are so fucking terrible, why don't you try to make a good one instead of bitching about it?" So I've been trying to carve out half-in, half-out of the mainstream ideas for genre films made with some amount of care and intelligence and humor—to see if we can get back to that period we all liked in American cinema 25 years ago.

Soderbergh's Starpower

SCOTT AND BARBARA SIEGEL/2000

DIRECTOR STEVEN SODERBERGH HAS FASCINATED and bedeviled serious filmgoers for more than a decade. He arrived on the cinema scene like a comet, brightening the celluloid sky at the age of 26 with *sex, lies, and videotape*. Robert Redford might have founded the Sundance Film Festival, but Soderbergh, with his audacious independent film, put it on the map. The movie went on to win the Palme d'Or at the 1989 Cannes Film Festival, making the first-time feature film director the youngest ever to take home that award. An international critical and commercial hit, *sex, lies* seemed like the calling card of a major new talent.

And it was. Except Soderbergh could not, for the longest time, find the commercial lightning that had struck him back in the late 1980s. *Kafka* (1991) divided critics and found no audience. *King of the Hill* (1993) was a much-admired movie, but its critical adulation did not translate at the box office. The *noir*-ish *The Underneath* (1995) was an attempt at a more commercial genre, but it went nowhere. *Gray's Anatomy* (1996) and *Schizopolis* (1996) were both narrowly focused films that were not designed to reach large audiences, not even on the art-house circuit.

Then, nearly a decade after he burst upon the scene, his career suddenly took off afresh. Known all that time as Steven (*sex, lies, and videotape*) Soderbergh, he finally had a new middle name: *Out of Sight* (1998).

Sitting and talking with Soderbergh in a New York hotel suite on the eve of the release of his latest film, Universal's *Erin Brockovich*, starring Julia Rob-

From *Film Journal International*, March 2000, Reprinted with permission.

erts and Albert Finney, the director recalls the turning point in his career, saying, "I was ready for a new middle name. That was a really important film for me to do, and an important film for me to do well because it was a very public piece. If I blew it, it was gonna be really difficult for me. In terms of self-imposed pressure, that was the most I ever felt. Not because other people were putting it on me, but because there was no room for error."

Soderbergh had gotten into the position of needing *Out of Sight*, he says, "because of the choices I made." But he has no regrets about his career path. "Had I not made all those movies prior to *Out of Sight*, I wouldn't have made *Out of Sight* the way I did. And that was important. Some people don't understand that process. I'm lucky that I had the luxury to make those things first, but I was definitely feeling that I was marginalizing myself. I didn't mind being an art-house cult failure, but I didn't want to spend my entire life there."

There was, Soderbergh admits, something romantic about the arc of his career up to that point. "There was a part of me that was sort of comfortable disappointing people. I was reveling in that. But at a certain point, I thought: I like all kinds of movies. And I was disconcerted by the fact that 50 percent of my filmmaking opportunities were being limited because nobody was considering me for things that weren't strict art-house fare."

Soderbergh was making *Out of Sight* when his producers first broached the subject of his directing *Erin Brockovich*. When they pitched it to him, he recalls telling them, "That sounds awful!" Later, however, while finishing up his next effort, the critically acclaimed *The Limey* (1999), he chanced to pick up the script of *Brockovich* and finally read it for the first time. "I loved her," he says, describing the real-life heroine who was responsible for getting the largest settlement ever paid ($333 million) in a direct-action lawsuit in U.S. history. He was drawn to directing it, he says, because "it was unlike anything I had made before; I wasn't sure I could pull it off. There needs to be a section of the pie that's sheer panic to keep you energized. I just thought, it's not an easy movie to make, and to do it well and to do it right is going to be a challenge."

Julia Roberts was already attached to the film when Soderbergh came aboard. When asked if, at the end of the day, *Erin Brockovich* is a Julia Roberts movie or a Steven Soderbergh film, the director smiles. "It's a Julia Roberts movie," he says. "That's how I describe it to people. I just thought she's going to be great in this part. There aren't many roles like this around [for an actress], and she's the perfect person for it. It was as smooth and as pleasant an experience as I've had with any actor, and she's in every scene of the film. She was a dream. I think she's at the absolute peak of her talent," he adds, "and I think she's in a good place personally—all of that seemed to contribute to her being ready."

And Soderbergh was ready, as well. He took this massive story about more than 600 plaintiffs and found its through-line. Taut and trim, the movie has a surprising pace to it. Soderbergh had begun his career as an editor and his ability to stylishly tell a story owes much to his early training. "It [editing] is something I think about as I'm developing the movie," he reveals, "and especially as we're shooting it. I'm always looking for ways that are more efficient, or more elegant than the norm, to put information across or to create a feeling. On *Erin Brockovich,* which superficially is a very linear, straightforward film, there are still a lot of little things in it that come out of my being preoccupied with that element of moviemaking.

"Certainly, for a movie with Julia Roberts in it, there are jump cuts, and things that you don't normally associate with her," he continues. "At the same time, I very much didn't want to do things that were out of line with the story I was trying to tell, because Brockovich is such a direct person that I didn't want to get fancy." Nonetheless, editing turned out to be the key to telling this story. "The first cut was really long [three hours and 15 minutes]." Ironically, however, Soderbergh was the one who kept fighting to shorten the film. "I'm usually trying to cut stuff out and the producers are trying to have me leave stuff in," he says. "I'm all for making movies shorter if I can. That's the way I like it. I don't know where that comes from; it's not that I'm impatient. I just think you've got to earn that. If you go much over two hours, I think you really better have a good reason."

There are echoes of last year's commercially disappointing John Travolta vehicle, *A Civil Action,* in *Erin Brockovich,* but Soderbergh isn't bothered by the comparison. "The difference between the two films," he explains, "is that this is not a movie about a lawsuit, this is a movie about a woman who got involved in a lawsuit. So, there are no courtroom scenes, except one, and nothing that can't be understood by the lay person. The good news is Erin is us. She's not a lawyer, not a scientist, not a toxicologist, so things have to be explained to her in a way that we would understand. That allows the audience in without feeling condescended to. I also knew that we had a happy ending." He laughs.

And why shouldn't he laugh? He's already lined up his next two projects: The first is a Fox Searchlight film called *Traffic* that is scheduled to begin shooting on April 2. And in January 2001, he begins a remake of *Ocean's 11* that will star George Clooney, Brad Pitt, and possibly Julia Roberts. "We're talking to a lot of people," Soderbergh says. "There are ten great parts in it and we're trying to work out a situation where we get ten big people. The original film," he adds, "was not great, but we've got a great script. We've taken the basic idea and completely changed it. It's going to be really fun." By that time, Steven (*Out of Sight*) Soderbergh might well become Steven (*Ocean's 11*) Soderbergh. In the meantime, he's poised to be Steven (*Erin Brockovich*) Soderbergh. What's in a (middle) name? In Hollywood, it's usually at least $100 million.

Steven Soderbergh: From *sex, lies, and videotape* to *Erin Brockovich*—A Maverick Director's Route (with Detours) to Hollywood Clout

ANNE THOMPSON / 2000

Steven Soderbergh keeps up with the details. He likes footnotes, whether he's reading David Foster Wallace or writing his own in his most amusing book, *Getting Away with It, Or: The Further Adventures of the Luckiest Bastard You Ever Saw.* He promptly answers his e-mails on his Power-Book—even now, while he's juggling finishing the edit on *Traffic,* writing his adaptation of Stanislaw Lem's space classic *Solaris,* making notes for the sequel *Son of Schizopolis,* and prepping his next, *Ocean's Eleven.*

It's hard to imagine that this bespectacled egghead was once a Little League pitching ace who threw no-hitters and hit .500. ("I was in the zone," he says.) Now he's in an equally rarefied zone: that of Hollywood's A-list directors. Soderbergh is three-for-three with *Out of Sight, The Limey,* and *Erin Brockovich,* whose star Julia Roberts, is heading into Oscar season as a Best Actress front-runner. Finally, the movie world is figuring out that Soderbergh is an actors' director ("I happen to like them," he says.) Performers from Andie MacDowell (*sex, lies, and videotape*) to George Clooney (*Out of Sight*) to Terence Stamp (*The Limey*) have done their best work with him. And his cachet among actors is such that his upcoming update of the Rat Pack curio *Ocean's Eleven* attracted an almost unheard-of collection of A-list talent, including George Clooney (who's also producing), Brad Pitt, Julia Roberts, Matt Damon, and Bill Murray. "His real signature is that he brings out the

From *Premiere Magazine,* December 2000. Published with permission from *Premiere* Magazine. Copyright © 2000, Hachette Filipacchi Magazine, Inc.

best in all his collaborators," says screenwriter Howard A. Rodman (TV's *Fallen Angels,* for which Soderbergh has directed an episode). *"Erin Brockovich* would have been a movie-of-the-week in anyone else's hands."

The director's he reveres range from Richard Lester (*Getting Away with It* features an exhaustive Q&A with the director of *A Hard Day's Night*) to Jean-Luc Godard. Giant posters of such Godard rarities as *Les Caribiniers* and *Bande á Part* dominate Soderbergh's Burbank office. "Godard is a constant source of inspiration," he says. "Before I do anything, I go back and look at as many of his films as I can, as a reminder of what's possible." But the director Soderbergh probably resembles most is that master of many genres, Howard Hawks, who cannily, craftily improved just about every story he got his hands on.

Ever since Soderbergh arrived on the scene in 1989 with the $1.2 million Sundance smash and Cannes Palme d'or winner *sex, lies, and videotape* ("a film about deception and lost earrings"), the writer-director has avoided letting Hollywood's overheated praise go to his head. For one thing, he labored for years in Hollywood and in his hometown, Baton Rouge, Louisiana, as a worker-for-hire on TV game shows, music videos, documentaries, and after-school specials, honing his skills as a writer, editor, and director. He's also intensely self-critical. He was not only willing to reveal himself in the semi-autobiographical *sex, lies, and videotape* and *Schizopolis*—the latter film starring himself, his then-wife Betsy Brantley, and their daughter, acting out their family life—but he recognizes that the artier experiments *Kafka, The Underneath,* and *Schizopolis* were less than satisfying to audiences. Yet he insists that those three features and his six short films were crucial to his own growth. "He's an authentically gifted, idiosyncratic filmmaker," says producer Ron Yerxa (*King of the Hill*). "He's not afraid to fail. And he doesn't kiss anyone's ass."

Soderbergh's latest radical move has been to join Los Angeles Local 600 as a card-carrying cinematographer. Having operated his own camera on his shorts and on *Schizopolis,* Soderbergh decided to be his own cinematographer on the drug drama *Traffic,* his "$49 million handheld Dogma film." Not surprisingly, the ensemble movie—which stars Michael Douglas, Catherine Zeta-Jones, Dennis Quaid, Don Cheadle, and Benicio Del Toro—has the raw immediacy of a documentary. Soderbergh tried to get the screen credit "directed and photographed by," but the Writers Guild wouldn't give him a waiver to put the "photographed by" credit between the writer's and the director's credits, and he was unwilling to credit himself twice. So, using his late father's first two names, he concocted the pseudonym Peter Andrews for the cinematographer. Will he also shoot the glossy studio picture *Ocean's Eleven?* "I don't think you can go back," he says. "You feel so close to the movie when you shoot that it would be hard for me now to insert someone into that process."

PREMIERE: *It's difficult to find a thematic thread in your films; you're a bit of a chameleon.*

STEVEN SODERBERGH: Good. You know, there are two kinds of filmmakers. There are filmmakers who have a style. And they look for material that fits that style. I'm the opposite. I look at the material and I go, "Okay, who do I have to be to put this across?"

PREMIERE: *Many of your characters are spinning out of control and then find their way, from James Spader in* sex, lies, and videotape *to George Clooney in* Out of Sight *and Julia Roberts in* Erin Brockovich.

SODERBERGH: Protagonists in my films tend to be at odds with their surroundings and/or the people around them. This is what I liked about Erin. She was more interesting than a fictional character. Somehow, when you're writing fiction, it's hard for the characters and the situation not to seem constructed. Erin was there full-blown and she drove the narrative, and you thought, "ok, now what? What is she going to do?" Because she can be as self-defeating as she can be successful. You have to work back from that and say, "What's the best way to put her and the story across?"

PREMIERE: *You brought more realism to that film than your average studio director would have. At the same time, you were working with a major star. When you looked at Roberts's work every day, did you see what a star brings to a movie?*

SODERBERGH: God, yeah. She was ready to go. She was on the blocks, day one. It was a great time to get her. I'd look at dailies and understand why she was a star and why she has the career she has and that you can't—though we do—put a price on it. Some people have it and some people don't. She's got it—a lot.

PREMIERE: *Clooney's coming along as a producer-star. You're working together on* Ocean's Eleven.

SODERBERGH: He's got all the tools. There's nobody like him around his age, who has the kind of vibe that he has. He's a man. He's not a boy. George's thing is, "I don't need any more money; what I want is a legacy of movies I can look back on and feel good about." He's very pragmatic, smart. He knows why he makes the choices he makes, and he understands dispassionately the result.

PREMIERE: *Warner Bros. sent both you and Clooney the* Ocean's Eleven *script?*
SODERBERGH: We got sent it simultaneously without knowing that each had been sent the script. I called Warners back the next day and said, "I want to do it" And Lorenzo [Di Bonaventura, Warners' production chief] goes, "That's good, because George read it and he wants to do it."

PREMIERE: *So you and George worked out the deal structure?*
SODERBERGH: Our whole deal was, "Remember those Irwin Allen [producer of *The Poseidon Adventure, The Towering Inferno,* et al.] movies with 15 stars—wouldn't that be cool?" There's only one way to do it: Come up with a formula that everybody adheres to. And the bottom line is, nobody's getting what they normally get, up-front [salary] or in the back-end [share of the revenues]. The studio said, "This is how much back-end you can have." It's a slice of a certain size, and we all said great. It was led by George, and Brad [Pitt] and Julia [Roberts] said, "We're in."

PREMIERE: *The film noir* The Limey *was designed as a vehicle for Terence Stamp, complete with footage from his 1967 film, Poor Cow.*
SODERBERGH: [Writer Lem Dobbs] and I decided on him before we did any work, which was great, and so when I called him on the phone, I was very anxious because I didn't know him. I didn't even know anybody who knew him, or what I was in for, but I wanted him and luckily he wanted to do it. He's a dreamboat.

PREMIERE: *While the storytelling in* The Limey *is quite innovative, your next picture,* Erin Brockovich, *was a more conventional crowd-pleaser.*
SODERBERGH: *Erin Brockovich* is not the place to be standing between the audience and the movie screen, waving your arms. Coming off *The Limey,* I wanted to try a different discipline that was really pleasurable. I thought, "I

need to let my interest in fragmented narrative go for a while," and *Erin* just seemed like the perfect antidote. And then coming out of that, I was ready to do something a little harder.

PREMIERE: *What attracted you to* Traffic *which you made at USA Films after the major studios passed?*
SODERBERGH: Back in '96, I was thinking about drugs, like, what role do they have in a person's life, and culturally, what are the reasons for the way we view them the way we do? So it was in my mind that I didn't want to make a movie about addicts. When I found out that Laura Bickford owned the rights to the *Traffik* [British Channel 4 TV] miniseries, I said, "I know what to do with that." And we started that process.

PREMIERE: *Why was it so hard to set up? Stephen Gaghan's script read like an accessible thriller, like Costa-Gavra's* Z.
SODERBERGH: You're stoned! Oh, it's compelling, but it was hard for me to describe what it was like and who the audience was going to be. I was hard-pressed to come up with a drug movie that had made money. And it's long: two hours and 20 minutes. Most people haven't seen *Z*, which was the model we were using. It's not an unreasonable thing for someone who is spending $49 million to ask, "Can you give me a taste of what's in store?" So I talked about things like *The French Connection*.

PREMIERE: *Harrison Ford was originally slated to play* Traffic's *role of the drug czar whose daughter is hooked on drugs; he then stepped out, and the role was taken by Michael Douglas. What happened?*
SODERBERGH: This was something very different for [Ford]. I talked about how I'd like to work with our run-and-gun approach, that in addition to operating [the camera] I would be the director of photography and there would be a lot of available light and it would be moving really quickly. And with two cameras, he would spend more of his day acting than any other movie he'd been on. He seemed very jazzed by that. But I also knew that this was not a slam dunk. He never said, "I'm in and I'm doing it." While this process was going on—and the deal by which he would take $10 million, half his usual price, which he was totally open to, was being conceptualized—we fixed Robert [the character Ford was to play] and found a way to make him the emotional center of the movie. And [then] he said, "I don't feel like this

is what I want to do right now." I wished it were otherwise, but I'm a big believer in instinct. If something's holding him, do you want an actor on the set who doesn't want to be there?

[For his part] Michael Douglas really enjoyed being able to spend most of his day working instead of waiting. There were a couple of key emotional scenes where we were moving so quickly that it enabled him to stay right there, and there would be a break of two minutes between one angle and the next. I was really impressed, performance-wise, at how readily he fell into the low-key, naturalistic approach that I was trying to maintain. It's not a movie-star performance. It's a very secure performance, and it comes from someone who doesn't have to show off anymore.

PREMIERE: *You shot this movie yourself, mostly, using a handheld camera, which must have been logistically complex, given that the picture has 110 principal roles and was filmed in nine cities. Why do this project that way?*
SODERBERGH: I'd been refining the idea of doing a run-and-gun movie over the last couple of films, trying to make things more naturalistic, and this seemed to be the one to do it on, because of the subject matter, the size, and the short schedule. Shooting this way helped us to be able to get it done in 54 days, [with] what started as a 165-page screenplay. And the momentum was maintained from beginning to end, which is great for the actors.

[As for doing the cinematography myself], it was a natural progression. I was trained as a still photographer. I shot my short films, and *Schizopolis*. I watched the [cinematographers] whom I worked with very closely—too closely, probably, for them. It's very comfortable for me.

PREMIERE: *You easily could have filmed it as a more glossy, conventional thriller, with a boom-boom pace and music pumping. Your way is more daring.*
SODERBERGH: The riskier thing would be to do it the other way. What you're selling is that we're giving you a snapshot of what's going on right now, and if it doesn't feel like that, then the people are going to check out. Any attempt to gloss it up would be rejected, whether consciously or subconsciously. The intent of the film didn't line up with that sort of traditional Hollywood film approach.

PREMIERE: *Are moviegoers tired of the same old formulas?*

SODERBERGH: They're tired of all the same movies that feel like they were directed from the back of a limousine. I know I am.

PREMIERE: *Is that the reason so many filmmakers, such as yourself or even a more traditional Hollywood filmmaker, like Joel Schumacher, are becoming interested in the ultra-realistic Dogma-style moviemaking philosophy?*
SODERBERGH: It's used in an attempt to get at something that feels emotionally honest and immediate. There are similar things happening in writing right now. I'm intrigued by what Dave Eggers [*A Heartbreaking Work of Staggering Genius*] and David Foster Wallace [*Infinite Fest, Brief Interviews with Hideout Men*] are up to because it's in service of trying to get at an emotion. Eggers's book wouldn't be as powerful if it weren't so deconstructed. For the first time since I can remember, somebody has written a book in that format that is actually moving. And Wallace is after the same thing. It's going on quietly, but I think it's a huge thing. In movies, the formal choice has to be appropriate to the material. I'm trying to sort out now how much of that feeling I can bring to a movie like *Ocean's Eleven,* which is very stylized. You derive a certain pleasure from the artificiality of watching a big caper movie with a bunch of movie stars. And I need to be careful not to subvert it needlessly and piss the audience off, because they want to be entertained. [But by the same token] you have to resist the impulse that when you have a movie of a certain size with certain people in it, you must execute it in a way that is consistent with how those movies are normally done. If I have Michael Douglas, then I have to do it a certain way, because that's what people will want—I don't think that's true. I think if you do something that is consistent with the intent of the material, people will go in whatever direction you want.

PREMIERE: *Sometimes too much realism can be a problem, as was the case with Clooney and Jennifer Lopez's infamous trunk scene in* Out of Sight *as you originally shot it.*
SODERBERGH: With everybody encouraged to be auteurs, [directors] tend to not talk about the importance of people like [*Out of Sight* producers] Jersey [Films]. I was bouncing everything off these people, I got notes from them. My idea was that by shooting this lengthy scene in a single take, the sense of emotional proximity would be increased. You were sharing their experience exactly—you were in there with them for the same amount of time as they

were. And then it would be great to watch the emotional ebb-and-flow of the scene uninterrupted. The Jersey people knew I was wrong. They would just smile. So a day and half, 45 takes later, you watch it in dailies, and as a self-contained shot, it works. It's like a short film. My belief is that the period between when you know you're going to get together with somebody and when you actually get together is the most electric—we know it's going to happen, and then we have to wait for it to happen. I was trying to elongate that for as long as I could. And I had two performers who understood that. It was only when I watched it in context with the rest of the movie that I realized how wrong I was. It was so obvious when I had our first preview. It was comical how the audience literally turned on the movie at that point. It just ground the film to a halt. What I should have understood is that every time you cut away and came back, you bought so much, because the audience filled in the gap for you.

PREMIERE: *After* sex, lies, and videotape, *Hollywood anointed you the next big thing. Robert Redford and Sydney Pollack asked for meetings. But you followed* sex, lies, *with* Kafka, *an $11 million art film!*
SODERBERGH: That was all calculated. I wanted to try a lot of different stuff, 'cause when you start out, you feel like, "I can do anything." It takes you a while to realize, "No, you can't do anything. In fact, here are the things you do well, and here are the things you don't do well." [As far as *Kafka* is concerned], I don't do well with material that is inherently cold. The experience of it I wouldn't trade for anything: I got to work with Alec Guinness and Jeremy Irons, and Prague was amazing. Going from *Kafka,* to *King of the Hill* was a result of my wanting to have the experience of making a picture that was a little warmer.

I'm good at finding a piece—whether it's *Out of Sight* which is a melodrama, or a star-crossed romance—and finding a way to make that story satisfying for an audience, so that they don't feel like they're getting hit in the forehead with the points that you're trying to make. I'm a good neutralizer for material that could very easily tip over into being just obvious or irritating or pedestrian. You come up and you realize, "Okay, I'm not Fellini. [*Laughs*] I'm not one of those people who come along and alter the landscape."

PREMIERE: *But you did—*sex, lies, and videotape *actually altered the indie-film landscape.*

SODERBERGH: Because *sex, lies, and videotape* made a lot of money at a time when films like that were not making any money; that's why we're talking about it today. If it had made half a million dollars, things would be very different right now for me. [*Laughs*] That movie bought me so many mistakes. It bought me the luxury of being able to make *King of the Hill* and *Kafka*.

PREMIERE: *In the case of* The Underneath, *a little-seen caper film you made in 1995, you thought it was a disaster even as you were making it.*
SODERBERGH: I knew it before we started. But I want to be very careful here not to denigrate the efforts of everybody who worked on that movie. Nobody knew that while I was making it, I was miserable, and that I felt it was a broken-backed idea to begin with and that I had not been rigorous with the material and I had not come up with a way to make it distinctive. I disconnected so far from the excitement that made me want to make movies. It took sitting on a set and wondering if I wanted to be on a set anymore to shake me awake. And so in many ways, it was the most important film that I made.

I woke up one day and said, "If you feel you've lost yourself, then you need to retrace your steps." And so I literally went about recreating the conditions in which I made my early short films. I thought, "I'm gonna go back home, get five people together"—four of them were the ones I grew up with, making films—"and I'm going to start over." And we made *Schizopolis*. It was like my second first film. I think everything since then has been much more fun to sit through.

I was a baseball pitcher as a kid, and I was really good, and then I woke up one morning. I was 12, at my peak, and I didn't have it anymore, whatever that thing is that makes you know that you're better than the other guy. I still had the technical skills, but that thing was gone. It was an overnight thing—the next game I played, I got hammered, and I never recovered. I knew when I woke up that morning when I was a kid—I knew that it was over, that I didn't have it. When I had that experience while making *The Underneath,* the feeling was different—because I understood that I could get it back.

Having Your Way with Hollywood, or the Further Adventures of Steven Soderbergh

DENNIS LIM/2000

ALTERNATELY CREDITED AND BLAMED for single-handedly inventing the American independent film as we know it (with a little help from Miramax, Sundance, and the Palme d'Or), Steven Soderbergh spent the '90s distancing himself from *sex, lies, and videotape.* Or rather, from the catch-all icon, deathless tabloid headline, and generational albatross that his precocious first feature soon became. He embarked instead on a quietly prolific career notable for its chameleonic about-turns and willful resistance to anything that might be regarded as repetition. In 2000, with the calm resolve and authority that has bolstered his recent work, Soderbergh once again stared down Hollywood, and this time emerged triumphant.

It's not just that he had two high-profile studio features in a calendar year (right now there's comparatively little fuss over Robert Zemeckis's *What Lies Beneath* and *Cast Away*), but that they both rank among the five or so most widely lauded Hollywood releases of 2000. The Julia Roberts vehicle-cum-crusading Norma Rae inspirational *Erin Brockovich* has grossed $125 million domestically (his biggest commercial success to date). Released last week to rapturous reviews, *Traffic,* an ambitious, tough-minded panorama of the disastrous War on Drugs, has been scooping up critics' prizes by the armful. It's likely that both movies will wind up on the Oscar shortlist next month; Soderbergh, for that matter, could be the first filmmaker to battle himself for directing honors since Michael Curtiz was nominated for *Angels with Dirty Faces* and *Four Daughters* in 1938.

From *Village Voice,* January 9, 2001. Reprinted by permission.

In more concrete terms, *Traffic* is Soderbergh's fourth film in three years, and it caps a prodigious winning streak that began with the neo-noir smolder of 1998's Elmore Leonard caper *Out of Sight,* perhaps the sexiest Hollywood movie of the '90s, and continued with the following year's splintered reverie *The Limey,* which ingeniously enlisted Terence Stamp's still-magnificent visage to transfigure a vigilante thriller into a memory-saturated lament. The most gifted and fleet-footed genre deconstructionist of his generation, Soderbergh is also one of the very few American filmmakers working today who sees reinvention as the lifeblood of his craft. After years of apparently perverse career choices, the payoff—it's now evident—is considerable: Soderbergh straddles Hollywood and the indies with remarkable ease and on his own idiosyncratic terms, not least because his résumé implicitly rebuffs the lazy habits and restrictive conventions of both spheres. In the ultimate irony, this onetime wild card has, for now, reinvented himself as a sure thing, an attractive hire for studios for a host of increasingly obvious reasons: speed and economy, an uncanny track record with career-making performances (his knack for casting is matched by an unfailing generosity with actors), a newfound populism (or at least a newfound ease about his latent populism) merging profitably with his abiding restlessness and longstanding taste for quirk and foible.

Soderbergh assesses his evolution with characteristic bluntness: "I'm no longer a control freak," he declares. "The implementation of whatever aesthetic I choose for each film is as considered and systematic as it used to be, but I have a completely different way of doing it now. I used to be a perfectionist but it was the wrong kind of perfection. And I no longer think perfection is interesting—by definition it's not lifelike. On the set, it's really about refining your sense of what's important within a scene, and within the context of the film. You train yourself to start gravitating toward it, like a metal detector, and you let the other stuff roll down your back."

With more than 100 speaking parts and a relatively compressed 54-day shooting schedule, *Traffic* presented Soderbergh with his most daunting logistical challenge to date. "In the production meetings, I'd say, Look, what's most important is energy and emotion. Just be on your toes and be ready." To sustain momentum, the director shot the movie himself—a highly unusual choice for a production of its size and scale. "It's not often you get to be a trainee in such an important position on a $46 million movie," as he puts it. Soderbergh, whose cinematography experience had previously been limited to microbudget projects, says he plans to continue shooting all his films from now on, big or small. "I don't know that I could go back. Reinserting another person into the process would be awkward and frustrating."

Like Soderbergh's 1995 heist movie *The Underneath, Traffic* adopts stylized color coordination to steer viewers through a three-part narrative. "I was trying to push to look to its extreme, in each case, which is one of the good things about being your own DP," he says. "Occasionally my gaffer would go, 'Steven, I just want you to know that the window is 11 stops overexposed,' and I'd go, 'Yeah, I know.' That's just stuff you don't do if you want to get hired again, but that was also what made it fun." The burnished-brown Mexico segments were shot through filters and with a 45-degree shutter to create "a stroboscopic feeling," then digitally desaturated. In the San Diego portions ("to create an idyllic look that I thought would contrast nicely with the slimy undercurrent") Soderbergh employed a process known as flashing: overexposing the film to white light before the negative is developed. "It was very common in the '70s, pioneered by Vilmos Zsigmond," he explains. "It's used to its best effect in [Hal Ashby's] *Bound for Glory,* but you know, I'm not Haskell Wexler and I was fucking up a lot. It's not a very quantifiable process—what you were seeing through the lens bore no relation to what you were going to see on film."

Shooting handheld and with available light where possible, Soderbergh sought to cultivate an atmosphere of loose-limbed immediacy on set: "The aesthetic, combined with the fact that I was operating the camera, greatly reduced the number of things the actors had to block out." He acknowledges a certain kinship to the Dogme school. "I went through a similar psychic break myself, where I felt like formalism was a dead end. You could polish stuff into oblivion and strangle the life out of a movie. I realize Dogme's a gimmick, but I don't doubt its core of sincerity."

Soderbergh's immersion in the process is hardly a new development. He edited his first three features, and in fact, the role of editor seems a natural one, given his longtime fascination with narrative ellipses and time loops. But he suggests that the shift in emphasis, from postproduction to production, is instructive. "I haven't seen the early films in a while, but I'm curious to know if I shoot differently knowing I'm not going to cut it, whether I was protecting myself, or trying to make my life easier as an editor by shooting a certain way. On *Traffic,* I'd shoot any fucking thing and just think, you know, we'll sort it out later. On the early films, I'd be figuring it out in my head, like exactly how it was going to go together and I wouldn't leave the set until I knew, and that's a boring way to work. I'm more of a gearhead anyway. I just love camera equipment."

Traffic is hearty Hollywood entertainment with a social conscience (as is, to a lesser degree, *Erin Brockovich*), and Soderbergh, who worked closely with screenwriter Stephen Gaghan in adapting it from a British miniseries, says evenhandedness was vital. "I didn't want to come off like we had answers. The idea that some silly filmmaker after two years could sort it out would be outrageous. But there seems to be a huge vacuum in the public debate and I guess this is one of the few times I felt a movie could actually help. The funny thing is, everybody who sees it thinks it puts their point of view across, and I was expecting exactly the opposite. We had a screening in Washington for Customs, DEA, and the Department of Justice and they all came out saying they really liked it. The following night, there was some hardcore leftie NPR/PBS screening in L.A. and some guy stands up and goes, 'Thank you for making the first pro-legalization movie.' Then the other night, Commissioner Safir came to a screening and said he thought it was the most accurate representation of law enforcement he'd seen in a long time. And I have, you know, stoner friends who are going, like, 'Dude, yeah, great . . .' "

Soderbergh's commitment to roughing up his style coincided with a waning interest in autobiography. "I had come to the end of anything that I had to say about myself that was compelling, and I just got more interested in other people's stories. My last few films have not really been about me or anyone in my peer group, and I think they're much more interesting to sit through for that." *Out of Sight* is often cited as the movie that jump-started the Soderbergh renaissance, but the real resuscitation began with the two films he made back-to-back in 1995.

Burned out and disheartened after *The Underneath*, he retreated to his hometown of Baton Rouge, Louisiana, to "start over again, get in touch with the enthusiasm of the amateur." The results: *Gray's Anatomy*, a Spalding Gray ocular-disease monologue filmed with a frantic emphasis on the visual, and, crucially, one final riotous burst of quasi-autobiography, *Schizopolis*, which Soderbergh directed, wrote, shot, and starred in. Made with borrowed equipment and a five-person crew (all old friends), the anarchic experiment had exactly the galvanizing effect Soderbergh had hoped for. "I was so wrapped up in my own shit that I wasn't looking out the window. I was just hanging out in my own house with the blinds drawn and the music on and not answering the phone. *Schizopolis* was about detonating that house, blowing it up and putting myself in a position where I couldn't go back anymore."

An elaborate Möbius strip that entwines deranged semiotic games, doppelgänger metaphysics, and bawdy sketch comedy, *Schizopolis* (in this writer's admittedly minority opinion, the most undervalued American film of the '90s) is a funny, poignant psychodrama about (among other things) the fallibility and futility of communication, specifically the death of language in a relationship. At the time Soderbergh was not only reeling from his Hollywood misadventures but enduring a painful breakup and, as if to call attention to the personal subtext, he cast his soon-to-be-ex-wife, actress Betsy Brantley, and their daughter, Sarah, as his on-screen family in *Schizopolis*. "It probably crossed the line from personal into private filmmaking," he dryly remarks.

Via published journals, numerous interviews, even his *Schizopolis* persona, Soderbergh has over the years been subjected to a good deal more analysis—and self-analysis—than your average film director. His fairy-tale beginning ensured that backlash was encoded in the Soderbergh narrative—something the shellshocked 26-year-old neophyte must have recognized when he accepted the Cannes Palme d'Or in 1989 with the words: "Well, I guess it's all downhill from here." (Another semi-mythic early anecdote has Soderbergh's hero, Richard Lester, telling him in Park City: "It gets harder, you know.") Talk of impossible expectations, squandered promise, and even self-sabotage swirled around the defiantly ambitious *Kafka,* the Depression-era coming-of-age tale *King of the Hill,* and *The Underneath,* obscuring the fact that the films were never without merit and collectively represented a thoughtful, questing attempt to stay independent. Even in evaluations of the subsequent upswing, the director's psyche was central. As he was emerging from his crisis with *Schizopolis* and *Gray's,* the *Los Angeles Times* obligingly ran a huge profile headlined "The Funk of Steven Soderbergh." Promoting *Out of Sight* in the *New York Times,* star George Clooney theorized that the director suffered from a fear of success.

To complicate matters, Soderbergh is given to his own public displays of soul-searching. His latest book, *Getting Away with It, Or: The Further Adventures of the Luckiest Bastard You Ever Saw* (published a year ago in the U.K., just out here) flip-flops between thorough, insightful interviews with Richard Lester and journal entries over a 12-month period starting March 1996—a trying time during which Soderbergh worked with director Henry Selick on the screenplay for *Toots and the Upside Down House* (never made), polished scripts for schlocky thrillers *Mimic* and *Nightwatch* (barely seen), struggled to secure distribution deals for Gray's and *Schizopolis*, developed a project called *Human Nature* (written by Charlie "Being John Malkovich" Kaufman, since filmed by Michel Gondry), and looked for a paying job that would serve as his reentry to Hollywood (he settled, reluctantly at first, for *Out of Sight*).

Soderbergh's writing voice is a humorously exaggerated version of the chronically self-deprecating deadpan that he tends to deploy in conversation. (The diary that accompanies the *sex, lies, and videotape* screenplay is similarly wry, a success story narrated with mounting incredulity.) While the *Getting Away* journal is often surprisingly frank, its most revealing aspect may be the constant self-laceration, which eventually registers as protective irony; it's clear too that Soderbergh is aware—and somewhat disgusted—that the book exists ultimately as a form of self-promotion. (Unsurprisingly, the author of these endlessly reflexive, obsessively footnoted entries confesses to a David Foster Wallace and Dave Eggers fixation. "It's not just postmodern bullshit, but I think an attempt to get at something emotional.")

Soderbergh doesn't hesitate to name names in the journal (from studio honchos to film critics) and, though he's calmed down considerably, has never been afraid to ruffle Hollywood plumage. He got off to a spectacularly impolitic start, referring to Jerry Bruckheimer and Don Simpson in a *Rolling Stone* interview as "slime barely passing for human." He had a falling out with Robert Redford over *Quiz Show*, which Soderbergh was at one point supposed to direct, and *King of the Hill*, which Redford had initially agreed to executive produce. He later found himself in a protracted legal battle with superproducer Scott Rudin over the rights to the John Kennedy Toole novel *A Confederacy of Dunces* (the suit was eventually settled out of court in Soderbergh's favor).

Soderbergh is more comfortable in Hollywood now than he's ever been (though he's moving to New York once he completes his next film, *Ocean's Eleven*), and he says it's largely because he has a firmer handle on the pragmatics of the job. "I've gotten better at determining the key points in the process where I need to focus on incredible amounts of attention for a very short period of time." He says he performs better at pitch meetings too. "You want to create the impression that this train is gonna leave without them if they don't jump on. I think the sensation is probably that the trains that I'm talking about move a little faster than the ones I used to be talking about."

There may be a new confidence to Soderbergh, but even his most upbeat declarations are buried in self-effacement. "I was in my apprenticeship for some time and I guess I'm now finally open for business. You know, I was sort of working in the backroom, learning my craft, and now I feel, you know, OK, store's open, let's go, fire sale." His declining compulsion to serve as both writer and director played a part in reviving his career: "I'm not good at writing scripts for other people to direct, which only leaves me able to write for myself, and I can't generate an original screenplay every 18 months because I'm not interesting enough." All the same, Soderbergh says he's "really psyched" about his latest undertaking: He's midway through the first draft of a script for a remake of Tarkovsky's *Solaris* (to be produced by James Cameron), which will "return to the Stanislaw Lem novel and add several of my personal preoccupations." He's reluctant to get into specifics ("It's just going to sound awful") but says, "Conceptually it would be one of the most ambitious things I've attempted."

Meanwhile, he's working on a *Son of Schizopolis* project: "It's going to be even more out of control but will have a clearer narrative. The people who liked *Schizopolis* really responded to the energy and the fact that it threatens to derail every 30 seconds. If I graft that energy onto a narrative that's possibly moving toward something, people might dig it more." He's also developing a football comedy, *Leatherheads,* with George Clooney and plans at some point to adapt John Barth's *The Sot-Weed Factor.*

Soderbergh starts shooting *Ocean's Eleven,* a remake of the first Rat Pack movie, in February with a cast of heavyweights (Clooney, Pitt, Roberts, Damon). He's apprehensive about cinematography duties: "It's a much bigger film physically than *Traffic* and it requires a slicker look. Unfortunately I sense it's going to be a hell of a lot more fun to watch than it will be to make." Lewis Milestone's original, he concedes, was "more notorious than good. I can't be along in being somewhat agog that it was directed by the guy who made *All Quiet on the Western Front.* I mean, talk about range." But the new script, by Ted Griffin, is a substantial revamp. Soderbergh asserts, a little grandly: "*Ocean's Eleven* will be the apex of my yielding to whatever populist instincts I might have. This will be potentially the most indulgent I'll ever be toward that side of my personality."

On January 14, his 38th birthday, Soderbergh will be in town to collect his

Best Director award from the New York Film Critics Circle (which also gave *Traffic* its Best Picture prize). "It kills me that my dad can't see this," he says. His father, who died three years ago, was a Louisiana State University professor who enrolled Steven in a film class while he was still in high school; Soderbergh took his father's first two names for his pseudonymous cinematography credit on *Traffic*: Peter Andrews. "He was raised in New York, and to him it was the epicenter, the arbiter of everything. He would have gone out of his mind. I try and remember that. My dad would be levitating right now."

Soderbergh says he's still figuring out how to process the accolades after years of being the underdog. "There's no question that I'm more comfortable as a disappointment and not having people watch me. I will always be more comfortable in that position. I also recognize that it's very self-limiting, personally and professionally, and I have to find a balance somehow between my ambitions and my desires to keep my life and my world manageable." For now, he's steeling himself for the publicity glare of what promises to be a very busy awards season. "The problem is it totally takes you out of yourself, and that's something I have trouble with anyway—I don't need more things to contribute to that. But it's so fucking nice and I don't want to be a sad sack. When *sex, lies* happened, I martyred myself out of enjoying it. And you know, it's disingenuous and borderline offensive not to enjoy it. I'm going to try to this time."

Soderbergh on Soderbergh:

"This is the career I envisioned. I was very vocal early on that I intended to try a lot of different things and that I had no rules about who was writing the checks. It's an interesting group of films, some successful, some not, but there isn't a lot of repetition."

sex, lies, and videotape (1989) "Almost by definition, anything that people respond to with that kind of intensity is dated. Something was in the air that people connected to, and I wouldn't even pretend to know or attempt to analyze it—you'd drive yourself crazy trying to duplicate it."

Kafka (1991) "I wish I were older when I'd made it. I didn't have the chops yet to pull it off. It's just not fun enough; it was never intended to be really serious but that doesn't come across."

King of the Hill (1993) "It was an attempt to make a classical, straightforward narrative, and also in trying to stretch as a director, I'd always heard kids were a real chore, and I thought, well, let's try it. I wish it were grittier, but it's a solid piece of American filmmaking. It's the least European of the first four and that was part of its appeal: Can I strip myself of my Antonioni obsession?"

The Underneath (1995) "It's the coldest of the films I've made. There's something somnambulant about it. I was sleepwalking in my life and my work, and it shows. It offered some challenges in terms of fractured narrative that I was interested in, just not interested enough. The star of that movie, to my mind, is the cinematographer, Elliot Davis."

Schizopolis/Gray's Anatomy (1996) "One was an exercise in verbal and narrative abstraction, the other in visual abstraction, and both of them defined the edges and gave me a shape to work within that I hadn't had before. They've both informed every film that I've made since."

Out of Sight (1998) "The stakes are higher when you're playing in an arena of that size. There's more pressure, more people watching. But I think this helped me get over any fear I might have had because I had such a great time making it and people seemed to like it a lot. I came away feeling it was a good thing to have done."

The Limey (1999) "You could, without risking offense, call it a minor work. But it was important for me because of the opportunity it provided to experiment with narrative and indulge some ideas left over from *Out of Sight*."

Erin Brockovich (2000) "Like most people, I don't like to be lectured, so I was going strictly on my own instincts about how I want to be spoken to by a movie. You know, it's a *Rocky* movie, but the point was to make a good one, and that means not having a raised-fist courtroom scene at the end but finding a more oblique way to pay homage to the history of the genre."

Man of the Year: Steven Soderbergh
Traffics in Success

ANTHONY KAUFMAN/2000

YOU DON'T GET A BETTER or busier year in this business than Steven Soderbergh got in Y2K. While *Erin Brockovich* was breaking 100 million dollars at the box office, Soderbergh's 1999 release *The Limey* was still winning critical acclaim (with five 2000 Independent Spirit Award nominations). He was also beginning production on his tenth feature film, *Traffic,* an astutely interlaced story about drug trafficking, which starred newlyweds Michael Douglas and Catherine Zeta-Jones, and which he shot much of himself. *Traffic* went on to win a Best Picture nod from the New York Film Critics Circle, and Soderbergh received multiple awards and nominations from citywide and national critics associations all the way to the Hollywood Foreign Press (with two Golden Globe noms, for *Traffic* and *Erin Brockovich*). Last year also saw the publication of his second book, *Getting Away with It: Or: the Further Adventures of the Luckiest Bastard You Ever Saw,* which includes his own musings on his work, and conversations with British director Richard Lester (*A Hard Day's Night*). Lucky bastard? That, and a lot of skill.

But success has not spoiled Steven Soderbergh. He remains the same humble, self-doubting, and talented director that made *sex, lies, and videotape* in 1988 and consequently, "independent film" a household phrase. With each film, Soderbergh continues to take on new challenges, whether the fractured timeline of *The Limey,* the push-up bras of Julia Roberts, or the jigsaw puzzle of story and tone in *Traffic,* he continues to evolve as one of our most accomplished contemporary directors.

From *indieWIRE,* January 3, 2001. Reprinted with permission of the author.

Before the release of *Traffic* and right in the middle of prep for *Ocean's 11*—Soderbergh's adaptation of the 1960 Rat Pack classic—the Studio-Independent hybrid spoke extensively with indieWIRE's Anthony Kaufman about chasing the story, working as a D.P./director, shooting beneath a helicopter, his fickle experience with the Studios, and "controlled anarchy."

ANTHONY KAUFMAN: *So last night I saw* A Hard Day's Night *in preparation to talk to you and it occurred to me that* Traffic *is influenced by it, with the same sort of documentary feel. Would you agree?*

STEVEN SODERBERGH: There's the reportage aspect of the aesthetic, yes. . . . All of the Lester stuff is informing what I'm up to lately, along with a handful of other people. Always Godard. Anybody who is doing anything interesting is ripping off Godard in some way. For this film, I spent a lot of time analyzing *Battle of Algiers* and *Z*—both of which have that great feeling of things that are caught, instead of staged, which is what we were after. I just wanted that sensation of chasing the story, this sense that it may outrun us if we don't move quickly enough. And there's a lot of that in Lester's films, especially those from the 1960s.

AK: *This documentary approach that infuses* Traffic *is helped by you being behind the camera. Which leads me to the question: were you insane? It must just have been relentless working as director of photography and director.*

SS: It is. But it's so satisfying. Because you're getting what you want all day. I certainly underestimated the restorative value of being able to leave the set for 5 minutes, which you cannot do when you are your own cinematographer. Literally. I couldn't go to the bathroom until lunchtime. Because I had to sit there and make sure things we're going. Or we were shooting. Most of our day was spent shooting. The lion's share of the film is shot available light, so we showed up early, ready to shoot. But in this case, it felt so organic that it didn't really feel like I was doing another job. It felt very much like when I was making my short films. It was a very stripped down crew. It was really just: Let's show up and shoot.

My production sound-mixer who I've known since I was 13 and was one of the college students that I was hanging out with and making films with when I was growing up, sent me an e-mail when it was all done, saying, "This was the closest to what I imagined it could be like when we were making our own films and imagined making bigger films." This one, I felt like we finally captured . . . we transplanted that sense of work and play that we had in Baton Rouge 20 years ago on to this large-scale production. That was a nice note to get, because I had felt it too, because I think it translates. I know the actors like it.

A K : *How many people did you have on your crew?*
S S : There was me, a second-camera operator, the gaffer, the key-grip, even the grip and electric departments were only 3 deep each, so it was a pretty tight group. There's no video assists; none of that shit.

A K : *That's a bold decision, especially when now everyone is relying on stuff like the video assist.*
S S : *The Underneath* was the last time I used it. I threw it out. It was making me passive. Actors hate it. And it slows you down. I was willing to live with these accidents or things not being exactly the way I might do them, by not being able to see the monitor when I wasn't operating. To me, it was a trade-off that was always worth it. Starting on *The Limey,* I started operating. I shot and operated *Schizopolis,* but that doesn't count. In the case of *Traffic,* the other operator [Gary Jay] is somebody I've worked with before who is extraordinary. He's a guy that Michael Mann won't make a movie without. He's just unbelievably great. And I would often give him what I would con-sider the trickier stuff. He was usually on the longer lens, which by definition requires more decisions. And I would usually give it to him, because he's so gifted. He's been doing features for many years, but he came out of docu-mentaries. So his sense of composition within a realistic aesthetic is really pronounced. So I felt like we had the "A" team. We were, in basketball terms, what you would call a running team. And we had to be, considering the length of the script and the scale of the movie; it was a short schedule.

A K : *So you have this joke, this is your $45 million dollar Dogma movie. Were you paying attention to the other Dogma movies by Von Trier, and the others?*
S S : Since *Schizopolis* was shot in 1995 and not sort of finished until later, clearly, I had a similar turn. I don't know Von Trier; I've never talked to him. But I certainly felt that I was becoming a formalist and that's a real dead end. So I felt the need to break radically from that way of working, and clearly he did, too. Because his earlier films were machined to the point of insanity, unbelievable precision. Obviously, he just felt like that goes nowhere. Some

of the films are more interesting than others, but I like what they're trying to do. I thought *Celebration* was fucking great. Because it's done with an attempt to get at something. And it just fit in with my revisiting Richard Lester and trying to re-insert a sense of play in the films. And I think the films I've made since have been more fun to sit through.

AK: *And more fun to make?*

SS: That shouldn't matter. If that meant anything then *Cannonball Run* would be a great movie, because I'm sure it was fun to make.

AK: *In hearing about the production of this movie, it did occur to me and let me ask you: was this your most difficult undertaking?*

SS: Yeah, creatively and physically, it was the most demanding thing that we'd attempted. But it was not the most self-imposed pressure. *Out of Sight* was the most pressure I've felt under. Again, all self-imposed. There wasn't a sword hanging over my head. I felt that if I failed creatively to make an interesting movie out of *Out of Sight,* then I was going to be in big career trouble. It was a conscious attempt on my part to enter a side of the business that was off-limits to me, because I had marginalized myself. And I knew if I failed, I was fucked. It was balanced by the fact that I loved the material and I knew what to do with the material. But to block that out on the set every day and basically make decisions as though I was making *Schizopolis* and knowing if I failed that I was completely screwed, it's the equivalent of, "Be funny, Goddamn it!" So it was intense for me. I don't think anybody would have said they noticed that. But I got up every morning with knots in my stomach.

AK: *And with* Traffic?

SS: It just felt like it's going to be hard, it's going to call upon everything we have, every day, but I know what to do with this, it's the right time to make this movie. We've got a terrific screenplay, we've got a great cast, and when you have opportunities like this, you should take advantage of them and make the movie you want to make and don't look back. I wanted it to be good and I was concerned that it be good, but it was not like *Out of Sight.*

AK: *There's a couple stylistic things I wanted to ask you about. First, my favorite shot of the movie—and I was reminded of it while watching* A Hard Day's

Night—*is the helicopter shot. There's this interesting change of perspective and I wanted to ask you about how it came about?*

s s : There's two shots I like a lot, the one [helicopter shot] going over the presidential palace and then the upside-down shot of it landing. I was operating the one in the nose of the helicopter—the one of it landing was a remote head, because you cannot get underneath a helicopter. Because I asked! I think the reason they hopefully stick out in a good way is two-fold. It's probably the only undiluted lyrical passage in the whole film. For a minute the movie stops and is abstract for a second. And the score [by Cliff Martinez] is great there. And the second is that it's the first time that the camera is not eye-level. The whole movie the camera is at eye-level, purposefully so, so it really stands out. Technically speaking, [regarding] the upside-down shot, I knew I wanted it to be upside-down, because I was trying to hide the fact that we were shooting it in Los Angeles. So the initial plan was that the camera would just tilt up and the helicopter would just drop right on the camera. But on the second take, I told Gary Jay, the other operator who knows how to operate a geared head, try to follow the nose. Whatever he did, it totally worked, but it wasn't what we thought he was going to do. He ended up confused halfway through and ended up going the opposite way of the way he thought he was going, but he went with it anyway; but then we saw it on the [remote] monitor and it was great! It was an accident. Those are literally two of four shots in the whole film that I think, are not hand-held.

A K : *Were there any other miracle accidents, which always make a movie great. It feels like* Traffic *would be open to that.*

s s : Lots of little ones, whether its dialogue here or there, or near the end of the movie when Don Cheadle is thrown out of the house—the way he hits that guy in the chest—that was in the moment, that was not planned. You could tell the guy was not happy. Just that whole scene was a really good example of something on paper I was concerned about, because it read strangely. I knew it had to be there, but I was just a little worried about it, until I saw Don do it. And he totally made it. A lot of the stuff he was saying was just off the cuff. I've become a fan of not rehearsing stuff. And as soon as I saw a take, I knew it was going to be okay. He found a way in and that was my way in. And that's what you hope for everyday. You cast people that can do that.

A K : *You don't like rehearsing stuff? When did that happen?*
s s : I don't know. Because I used to be totally the opposite. I used to rehearse the shit to the point of exhaustion.

A K : *Do you think it has to do with your post-*Underneath *shift?*
s s : Yeah, a lot of it. And a lot of it is believing that life isn't ordered. And that nailing stuff down beforehand is not as interesting.

A K : *In the press notes, you speak of a "controlled anarchy"?*
s s : Exactly. What you're hoping for is a series of orchestrated accidents. It's scarier in a way, because you're not sure if something good is going to happen, but you just have to believe that the parachute will open. And it usually it does, if you've put the right group together. For me, it's just a much more satisfying way of working. But again, it's a radical shift from the way I started.

A K : *I just mentioned this post-*Underneath *idea. How do you feel about your career being categorized that way?*
s s : Oh, that's the way I feel about it. I haven't seen my earlier films in awhile, but my sense is that they are just not as much fun to sit through. I would rather sit through *Out of Sight* than the first four films. Just personally. If I had to leave one of them on the coffee table behind for you to watch, it would not be one of the first four. I was starting out. I was trying to figure out what the Hell I should be doing. I'm glad I spent the time trying to figure it out.

A K : *Now people are comparing you to people like John Ford and Howard Hawks. You're making movies really quickly, you're making them within the studio system, and you're making them in your own way. What's your reaction to that?*
s s : That's sort of the way the business has worked out. It's not surprising when you consider the independent movement, or whatever you want to call it, has been swallowed up by the studios, so it seems inevitable that I'd be some sort of hybrid. But you also have to, at some point, acknowledge what your capabilities are and what your limitations are. And if I turn out to be somebody who's better suited to making the kinds of films I've been making lately than art-house movies, then whatever. If you can't hit the 3-point shot, you should stop shooting 3-point shots, and learn how to drive the lane. So I'm just trying to play to my strengths. That doesn't mean I'm not

going to make stuff like *The Limey* or *Son of Schizopolis,* it just means I'm playing to my strengths.

A K : *Are there elements in* Traffic *that you're less confident about?*
s s : There's one aspect of every movie that scares you, or should, anyway. And consistency of tone was the issue in *Traffic.* Because there are three different stories and so many characters, everyone had to feel like they were in the same movie. And that was the trick. And I was going totally on instinct there. It wasn't until we got into the editing room that I would know whether we were successful. But that was the big pocket of fear: of suddenly having an actor or scene that felt like it was from another film.

A K : *There was something about tone, I read, where you talked about the difference between a "cold movie" and a "warm movie" and that you prefer the latter. But I feel that* Traffic *is a cold movie.*
s s : I don't. By design, it had to be a dispassionate movie in that it's trying to show you a lot of things without editorializing, but I also think, ultimately, it's also a very emotional movie by the time it lands. I hope it sneaks up on you. You've been watching things happen for a long time, and then in the last 10 or 15 minutes, it starts to settle. So I think you're right, the first 2 hours and 5 minutes of the movie, you could call "cold," in the sense that it's staring at things. And then my hope is that it would then shift warm and fuzzy mode.

A K : *What happened with getting* Traffic *produced. It starred at Fox, then went to USA Films, and I imagine you shopped it around some studios before?*
s s : Well, it was at Fox. What happened wasn't really surprising in that it was at Fox 2000, initially. But the person who was championing the project at Fox 2000 was gone by the time the first draft was ready. And the one person at Fox who was really, really passionate about it, Bill Mechanic, we now know, in retrospect, was not in a great spot to be green-lighting a movie like *Traffic.* Bill understood it, and got what the movie was about, but as we now know, it was a bad time for him and he was on the verge of leaving the company. We showed it to every studio in town and everybody said no.

A K : *Why do you think they said no, besides the obvious . . .*

ss: Besides the budget, the subject, the length, and the fact that there were no clear-cut good guys and bad guys, I don't know. From the get go, USA was saying, "We want in." And we were just testing the waters, and it turned out that they were the only people who wanted it.

AK: *I also wanted to ask you about working with Universal over the years. They have helped you out a lot with your films, from both sides of your career?*
ss: That's an interesting story in that I've made four films for them. And the first two [*King of the Hill* and *The Underneath*] were absolute money-losers. But I had a very good relationship and experience with Casey Silver, who was running the studio. And in spite of my track record, he was the one who called me and said, I want to send you this script, *Out of Sight.* They're talking to a lot of different people and you're not anywhere near the top of the list, but you could be, if you decided to pursue this, because I think you'd really be right for it. And he really backed me and got me that gig. And even though the film didn't make its money back, it was reviewed as a good thing for the studio to have done that year. It was something they were very proud of. And then when Casey got fired for making movies like *Out of Sight,* there was enough residual goodwill to carry over to *Erin* [*Brockovich*]. And that turned out to be the film that paid back Universal for my other three movies that didn't make their money. So I was really happy about that, because they really had been supportive and totally left me alone to make these things. And I don't like losing people money. I feel bad when millions of dollars are lost. I was just relieved when *Erin* performed the way it did, because I thought, we're even, they invested in me heavily, I've paid them back. Also, bear in mind, they were responsible for *Schizopolis.* They pre-bought video rights for enough money to make the movie, and then I paid them back when I sold it. Not many studios can lay claim to that, nor would want to, even. But I've never had a "directing deal." I have this producing thing going on with [George] Clooney now at Warner Brothers, but I was very specific about not having directing language in it, because I don't want to be obligated as a director to anybody.

AK: *You recently spoke about personal films, and you had said* Traffic *or* Erin Brockovich *are personal to you as much as say,* Schizopolis; *how is that?*
ss: People's definitions of "personal" when it comes to art are very odd, and to me exhibits a lack of understanding of what artistic process is. Because

I invest equally in all of these things. I don't necessarily think that "that really happened to me" is a criteria for whether something's good or interesting. So for the past few years, I've been more compelled by other peoples' stories than my own. That's just an outgrowth of my getting older. And I still make them the way they ought to be made and they still involve my interests and preoccupations, but they're just not about me.

A K : *What was your entry point for* Traffic?
S S : I was interested in drugs. And not just dealers and addicts. There's actually a brief passage in the Lester book, from 1995 or 1996, where I said, "I've been thinking about drugs lately, what role do they play in our culture and what do we do about them." It was clearly something that I was curious about. Because most people have had some exposure to them or know someone who's had some trouble. But I didn't know what form it would take, so I just filed it away. But it was very much something that I wanted to make a movie about.

A K : *What about* Ocean's 11?
S S : I'm prepping right now. It's a big one, physically big. Technically complicated on a level that I've never attempted before. I think it's going to be a hybrid of a slightly slicker aesthetic. More dollys, wideframes, I'm going to shoot Super-35. So a quotient of theatricality that I've moved away from, but still a very loose feel to it, still working with a lot of available light, still moving very quickly. I'm convinced that there's still an interesting mixture between these two very different aesthetics. I'm excited. I'm terrified. It's going to be very challenging, almost more than anything I've ever done. It's got me really anxious. It's just too complicated to now show up and know exactly what you're doing all day. It's a struggle. Because I tend to want to go, "We'll just get there. We'll figure it out." It's the kind of stuff that David Fincher can do in his sleep, but I don't think that way. I just don't think in three dimensions like that. Now I'm trying to train myself to think that way.

73rd Academy Awards

ACADEMY OF MOTION PICTURES
ARTS AND SCIENCES/2001

This transcript is taken from the backstage Q & A session between Steven Soder-bergh and members of the national press after his Best Direction Oscar win for Traffic.

QUESTION: *This is such an unusual thing to be nominated for two films in one year and for you to actually win. Were you actually surprised by this? Do you feel that* Erin Brockovich *has been orphaned by the* Traffic *win?*
STEVEN SODERBERGH: I think I looked pretty surprised, didn't I? All of you must know that I really didn't anticipate this. Didn't see it coming. I was having a great time, got to see a lot of my friends get up there, and was very happy already. But this is going to take awhile to process.

Q: *In the ceremony, you spoke about the importance of creating. You are considered one of the best independent directors and now you're arriving in Hollywood with this Oscar. How do you feel? Is this Oscar going to change you?*
SS: I've always followed the same methodology, from my first film up through the one I'm shooting right now. So I don't think I could alter my way of working or thinking, even if I tried. It's pretty ingrained. Certainly, coming up the independent route I didn't imagine this situation. But frankly, from the beginning, I've said that I don't delineate between studio films and independent films. I delineate between good movies and bad movies. And

25 March 2001. Transcript courtesy of the Academy of Motion Pictures Arts and Sciences.

we all would like to see good movies. And I don't care who is writing the check. I'm just going to keep plodding along and trying to stay busy.

Q : *Congratulations. Two terrific films, both very, very different. When you completed each film, was there a certain feeling that you had? Did you feel more strongly about one over the other?*

S S : No. Whenever people ask me which of your films is your favorite, I say the one I'm making right now. In the case of *Erin Brockovich* and *Traffic*, I was preparing *Traffic* while I was finishing *Erin*, and I was preparing *Ocean's 11* while I was finishing *Traffic*. So once I deliver them, I tend to move on mentally. I wish for the best, but as we know, you can't control what happens to these things once they go out there. Certainly, none of us anticipated what would happen to *Traffic*, because it was a difficult film to set up and one that we were told, time and again, had no commercial potential, so it was really exciting to see that the audiences went. That was a pleasant surprise.

INDEX

Conversations with Filmmakers Series
Peter Brunette, General Editor
The collected interviews with notable modern directors, including

Robert Altman / Theo Angelopolous / Bernardo Bertolucci / Jane Campion /
George Cukor / Clint Eastwood / John Ford / Jean-Luc Godard / Peter Greenaway /
John Huston / Jim Jarmusch / Elia Kazan / Stanley Kubrick / Spike Lee / Mike Leigh /
George Lucas / John Sayles / Martin Scorsese / Steven Spielberg / Oliver Stone /
Quentin Tarantino / Orson Welles / Billy Wilder / Zhang Yimou